PERFECT PASTA

PERFECT PASTA

MORE THAN 70 RECIPES FOR CLASSIC & MODERN DISHES

LAURA SANTINI

photography by
CHRISTOPHER SCHOLEY

RYLAND PETERS & SMALL

Senior Designer Megan Smith
Editors Kate Eddison and Alice Sambrook
Production David Hearn
Art Director Leslie Harrington
Editorial Director Julia Charles
Publisher Cindy Richards

Food Stylists Laura Santini and Kathy Kordalis
Prop Stylist Tony Hutchinson
Indexer Vanessa Bird

First published in 2017. This edition published in 2026 by Ryland Peters & Small
20–21 Jockey's Fields
London WC1R 4BW

www.rylandpeters.com
email: euregulations@rylandpeters.com

10 9 8 7 6 5 4 3 2 1

Text © Laura Santini 2017, 2020, 2026
Design and photographs © Ryland Peters & Small 2017, 2020, 2026

MIX
Paper | Supporting responsible forestry
FSC® C106563

ISBN: 978-1-78879-767-2

Printed in China

The author's moral rights have been asserted. All rights reserved. No part of this publication may be reproduced, stored in a retrieval system or transmitted in any form or by any means, electronic, mechanical, photocopying or otherwise, without the prior permission of the publisher.

CIP data from the Library of Congress has been applied for. A CIP record for this book is available from the British Library

The authorised representative in the EEA is
Authorised Rep Compliance Ltd.,
Ground Floor,
71 Lower Baggot Street,
Dublin, D02 P593, Ireland
www.arccompliance.com

NOTES

- Recipes in this book are based on 100 g/3½ oz. of uncooked dried pasta per person or 80 g/3 oz. fresh pasta per person.
- Both British (Metric) and American (Imperial plus US cup) measurements are included for your convenience, however, it is important to work with one set of measurements and not alternate between the two within a recipe.
- All spoon measurements are level, unless otherwise specified.
- Ovens should be preheated to the specified temperature. Recipes were tested using a fan oven. If using a conventional oven, follow the manufacturer's instructions for adjusting temperatures.
- All butter is unsalted, unless otherwise specified.
- All eggs are medium (UK) or large (US), unless otherwise specified. Recipes containing raw or partially cooked egg should not be served to the very young, very old, anyone with a compromised immune system or pregnant women.
- When using the zest of citrus fruit, try to find organic or unwaxed fruits and wash well before using.

contents

INTRODUCTION

This fabulous Fellini quotation is certainly true of my life, which has been filled with plenty of both, at home and at work. Just like rice, pasta is relatively cheap, and an inclusive blank canvas upon which cooks of all levels can combine pantry and passion to paint a carnival of flavours.

Pasta is for everybody; it is unifying and inclusive and can be as simple or as complicated as you want to make it. It is quick, easy, comforting and uplifting – it is so many things all tossed together in one little bowl.

When my publishers asked me to spill the beans on pasta and let the world into my three key pasta secrets, I was both honoured and excited.

Many times my non-cheffy friends have asked me why their pasta never comes out quite like mine. It is my hope that armed with these three key secrets, and over 70 delicious sauces, cooks of all levels will be released from stodgy, sticky meals and tossed with gusto into a world of al dente deliciousness.

'LIFE IS A COMBINATION OF **MAGIC** AND **PASTA**'

FEDERICO FELLINI

Way more than the sum of its simple parts, for me a good pasta is the ultimate expression of alchemy. The dishes in this book include my family's traditional, authentic Italian recipes going back several generations, which we serve at my restaurant Santini in London's Belgravia. These are combined with contemporary ideas and exciting twists such as the transformation of butternut squash and courgette/zucchini into spiralized boodles and zoodles. Wheat-free pastas are also widely explored and, I have to say, I have been beyond impressed by the fantastic quality and range of non-wheat pastas available out there. It used to be that non-wheat pastas would not hold their bite and end up a gloopy second-best. Thankfully, that is no longer true and today there is a perfect pasta to suit all tastes, diets and ages.

I really hope that you will enjoy cooking from this book as much as I have enjoyed writing it.

PASTA LA VISTA!

PASTA OVERVIEW

TRADITIONAL ITALIAN PASTA TYPES

Pasta secca (dried pasta)

In Italy, dried pasta is traditionally made from durum wheat or semolina flour and water. It can be cooked al dente, and uncooked it can last almost forever.

Pasta fresca (fresh pasta)

Italian fresh pasta is traditionally made using fine-milled 'tipo 00' flour and eggs. Fresh pasta is softer and wetter than dried pasta, so the cooking times are far shorter and it has a shorter life as it has to be stored in the refrigerator. The concept of al dente is quite different in this category, as you will never get that al dente 'bite'. Instead, strive to keep the texture firm and take care not to overcook it, as it will fall apart.

Pasta all 'uovo (dried fresh pasta)

Dried egg pasta falls somewhere in-between the two above. Fettuccine and tagliatelle in this category are brilliant and I personally prefer them because they come closer to al dente than the soft bite of fresh pasta.

Pasta secca senza glutine (gluten-free pasta)

All the big pasta manufacturers now have a comprehensive range of gluten-free dried pasta. This pasta is usually made with a combination of corn varieties and rice.

Integrale o farro (whole-wheat or spelt pasta)

Healthy eating has become a big global business and gluten-free pasta alternatives is a fast growing category in Italy. For those looking for healthful wheat alternatives, whole-wheat and spelt pastas provide a great middle-ground. The big manufacturers all offer whole-wheat options.

Coloured/flavoured pasta

There is a history of colouring and flavouring pasta in Italy. The most usual are spinach, tomato, beets, cacao, mushroom or squid ink. Other flavours include garlic, chilli/chile, red wine or herbs. A lot of the pasta alternatives come in great colours like red lentil and spirulina green, although some look better before cooking and sometimes lose their vibrancy when cooked.

Filled pasta

Because fresh pasta is soft, it can be folded and twisted into delicious pasta parcels, housing a variety of tasty fillings. Fresh pasta parcels generally have a very short life, not just because they are irresistible, but because the wet filling means they only last a day or so without ruining the pasta. There are also dried filled pastas, like my personal downfall, tortellini, which have been dried, along with their super umami-packed prosciutto and Parmesan filling. I love these cooked al dente in a simple chicken broth.

NON-WHEAT* PASTA ALTERNATIVES

Coeliacs and genuine intolerances aside, there has been a big shift in eating habits, and many today choose to either give up or limit refined carbohydrates and gluten. I have good news! Just because you don't or can't eat gluten, doesn't have to mean that you can't eat pasta.

Today, there are literally hundreds of new pasta alternatives that combine the healthful properties of legumes, grains and grasses into familiar pasta shapes ready to be tossed in yummy sauces. I have used a lot of these throughout this book, and have been both surprised and delighted by the fantastic textures and flavours this new world of healthful pasta offers. The abundance of these products online or in health food stores and supermarkets must mean only one thing: although some people are prepared to give up gluten and refined carbs, they are less ready to give up the comfort of a bowl of pasta. Below are some of the alternative pastas and noodles that I have come across while researching this book.

* **NOTE** Not all non-wheat pastas are gluten-free, so always check the label.

Grain pastas
Brown rice, oat, buckwheat, quinoa, rice and quinoa, corn, amaranth, sorghum, millet, white rice, teff, barley.

Bean and legume pastas
Chickpea, green pea, black bean, green lentil, red lentil, yellow lentil, cellophane noodles (mung bean flour).

Tuber, root and sea vegetable
Sweet potato, Jerusalem artichoke, cassava, potato, white sweet potato, yam, kelp.

Spiralized vegetables
Another fast-growing trend is to do away with all flour-based pastas (be they wheat or non-wheat alternatives) and replace with spiralized vegetables. Indeed most large supermarket chains now sell boodles (spiralized butternut squash, page 153) or zoodles (spiralized courgette/zucchini, page 34) in the same section as prepped stir-fry vegetables.

Yes, I bought a spiralizer, yes I tried it, yes I decided life was too short... cooking time is also tricky with these vegetable noodles and many stay more al dente if microwaved. If, like me, you do not have a microwave, I simply toss them in a non-stick pan just to heat them through but not cook them.

HOW TO MAKE FRESH PASTA & GNOCCHI

classic pasta dough

This simple recipe comes straight from Emilia-Romagna, the pasta-making capital of Italy. It is important to use proper finely milled pasta-making flour, which has 'type 00' flour or 'farina tipo 00' (doppio zero) on the packaging. In some parts of Italy, a tablespoon of olive oil is added for elasticity and flavour. Good free-range eggs are also important as they give the pasta a nice bright colour. In the UK, I use Burford Browns which have lovely sunny yolks. If your yolks are too pale, you can always add a very tiny drop of yellow food colouring to the pasta dough. Below is my basic recipe which has served me for years. This book is essentially about sauces and how to combine them with pasta, so please do not feel obliged to make your own pasta. However, if you do want to explore making fresh pasta in depth, 'Making Fresh Pasta' by Aliza Green is a great book.

500 g/3¾ cups 'type 00' flour, plus extra for dusting
½ teaspoon salt
5 eggs (the rule is 1 egg for every 100 g/¾ cup flour)

SERVES 4–6
(4 AS A MAIN COURSE, 6 AS AN APPETIZER)

Sift the flour into a mound on a marble board or clean work surface. Make a well in the centre, add the salt and crack the eggs in one by one.

Use a fork or your fingertips to beat the eggs lightly in the centre of the well, drawing in the flour a little at a time.

Note: Since eggs come in different sizes, your dough may be too wet or too dry. If too wet, add a little more flour; if too dry, add a drop of water.

When combined, knead together into a large ball of dough. It will look smooth, more like pastry than bread. Wrap in clingfilm/plastic wrap and leave to rest in a cool place for 15–30 minutes.

Once the dough has rested, if working by hand, lightly flour a rolling pin and get rolling until you have reached the desired thickness for your chosen shape. Roll either by hand or through the pasta machine until very thin and almost translucent, then cut into the required shape. If using a pasta machine, follow the manufacturer's instructions for your machine.

I recommend working with one-quarter of the dough at a time to make it more manageable.

sweet pasta dough

This sweet pasta is a great recipe to have up your sleeve. We serve these puffy pasta cookies covered in powdered sugar with coffee at Santini. In Italy, they are typically associated with carnivals and each region has a name for them. In Venice we call them 'galani', other parts call them 'chiacchiere', which literally means gossip. Whatever you call them, they are delicious!

430 g/3¼ cups 'type 00' flour, plus extra for dusting
2 eggs, beaten
20 g/1½ tablespoons soft butter, cut into cubes
65 ml/¼ cup white wine
2 tablespoons grappa
70 g/½ cup icing/ confectioners' sugar, plus extra for dusting
¼ teaspoon salt
1 litre/quart vegetable oil, for frying

SERVES 10–12

Mix all the ingredients (except the oil for frying) together in a stand mixer with the dough hook attachment.

When well mixed, remove the pasta dough from the mixer and knead until it's smooth, more like pastry than bread. Wrap in clingfilm/plastic wrap and let rest in a cool place for 15–30 minutes.

Once the dough has rested, if working by hand, lightly flour your rolling pin and get rolling until you have reached the desired thickness for your chosen shape. Roll either by hand or through the pasta machine until very thin and almost translucent. If using a pasta machine, follow the instructions for your machine.

I recommend working with one-quarter of the dough at a time to make it more manageable.

Cut the pasta into little rectangles, either with a knife or fluted pastry cutter. For the shape, imagine your pasta sheet is an A4/ letter-size piece of paper, you want to cut straight down the middle (portrait-side up) and then across in 4-cm/½-inch spaces.

Heat the oil in a large, heavy-bottomed pan and deep-fry in batches until golden, puffy pillows appear. Drain excess oil on paper towels. Dust with icing/ confectioners' sugar and serve.

classic fresh gnocchi

This book would not be complete without a recipe for gnocchi. I think everyone loves gnocchi. These light, fluffy potato pillows are best dressed with rich tomato or meat sauces or if you are feeling indulgent, the Gorgonzola and Walnut (page 58) would be dreamy. Raw gnocchi can be frozen on a tray and then, once solid, placed into bags for the future. You can cook them straight from frozen, so when I make them I triple this recipe and make a big batch.

1.3 kg/3 lb. floury potatoes (Désirée are perfect)
200 g/1½ cups 'type 00' flour, plus extra for dusting
1 UK large/US extra-large egg
a pinch of freshly grated nutmeg
a knob/pat of butter
salt

SERVES 4

Scrub the potatoes (with their skins on) and place in a large pan. Add 1 tablespoon salt and cover with plenty of cold water. Bring to the boil and cook for at least 30–40 minutes, until cooked through but not waterlogged. Check with a fork to ensure they are cooked right through to the middle (just like you need when you are going to mash potatoes).

Tip the flour onto a large, clean work surface.

Drain the potatoes and begin to peel while hot. You can do this by holding a hot potato on the end of a fork in one hand and using a small vegetable knife to peel off the skin with the other.

As soon as the potatoes are peeled, put them through a mouli or ricer so they become almost powdery. Add to the flour mixture.

Make a well in the centre of the potato and flour mixture, add the egg and a pinch of salt and nutmeg. Begin to draw all the ingredients together with your hands and knead for a couple of minutes until well combined into a smooth, soft, pillowy dough.

You do not want to overwork gnocchi dough as it will lose its lightness and become tough.

To make gnocchi, cut your dough into quarters. Flour your work surface. Roll the dough out one-quarter at a time into long sausages about 3 cm/1¼ inches in diameter and chop off thumb-size lengths, until you have used all the dough.

I like to roll each gnocchi over the rough side of a cheese grater or the back of a fork to give some sauce-catching texture.

Cook the gnocchi in a large pan of boiling salted water, just like pasta. Drop the gnocchi into the water, a small batch at a time (no more than ten pieces at once), and the minute they float to the top, remove with a slotted spoon. Place in the serving dish with the knob/pat of butter to stop them sticking together. Top with any of the hot cooked sauces in the book. Follow serving instructions for each recipe.

PANTRY PROPS

This is an ideal list of staple ingredients to keep in your store cupboard or fridge. They allow the rustling up of impressive and showstopping pasta dishes at the drop of a hat. That said, never forget that you can literally make a cover-worthy dish with just some olive oil, an old clove of garlic and a stock cube! Oh and a sprig of fresh rosemary is nice if you have it, but not essential...

shopping list

STORE CUPBOARD ESSENTIALS

- [ ] Extra virgin olive oil
- [ ] Dried pasta
- [ ] Garlic
- [ ] Onion
- [ ] Canned chopped tomatoes or canned whole San Marzano tomatoes
- [ ] Dried chilli flakes/hot red pepper flakes
- [ ] Anchovy fillets in oil* (the brown kind)* the only anchovies referred to in this book
- [ ] Sardines
- [ ] Tuna
- [ ] Tapenade
- [ ] Olives
- [ ] Capers
- [ ] Harissa or chilli/chili paste
- [ ] Pine nuts, pumpkin seeds, flaked/slivered almonds, walnuts
- [ ] Tomato purée/paste)
- [ ] Mushroom powder (ground shiitake, porcini, or mixed wild mushrooms, I use a coffee grinder)
- [ ] Toasted breadcrumbs or Pangrattato (page 16)
- [ ] Quick Aglio Olio Herb Seasoning (page 16)
- [ ] Oregano
- [ ] Wine
- [ ] Kimchi
- [ ] 'Nduja
- [ ] Rock salt
- [ ] Table salt
- [ ] Black pepper

FRIDGE USEFULS

- [ ] Butter (unsalted)
- [ ] Lemons
- [ ] *Fresh herbs:* Flat leaf parsley, basil, mint
- [ ] *Hard cheese:* Parmigiano Reggiano, pecorino, ricotta salata
- [ ] Bacon, pancetta, prosciutto, smoked salmon, mojama, bottarga
- [ ] Eggs
- [ ] Greek-style yogurt

Both of the recipes below are great pantry props and can be prepared when you have the time and inclination and then stored in an airtight jar for weeks. When you want something quick and tasty in the kitchen, just toss your hot drained pasta with good extra-virgin olive oil and a couple of tablespoons of either mix (or both!) and you will be well on your way to satisfaction.

You can buy good versions of these handy herb mixes in random duty-free shops. If you are not passing through Italy, it is very easy to mix up your own. I always keep an airtight jar of the Aglio, Olio Herb Seasoning in my pantry for a quick pasta fix; just add a spoonful of the mix and a splash of extra virgin olive oil to hot pasta and you are done. If you are in a real hurry you can just mix with olive oil and dip bread into it. Now you know nearly all my secrets...

quick aglio, olio herb seasoning

10 g/5 heaped tablespoons dried parsley (preferably freeze-dried so it is nice and bright)
10 g/1 tablespoon garlic granules
20 g/2 tablespoons dried chilli flakes/hot red pepper flakes
30 g/½-1 tablespoon salt flakes, to taste
½ teaspoon freshly ground black pepper

Combine all the ingredients well and store in an airtight container.

pangratatto

3 tablespoons olive oil
100 g/3½ oz. sourdough breadcrumbs
grated zest of 1 lemon
3 garlic cloves, crushed
3 tablespoons finely chopped flat leaf parsley
salt and freshly ground black pepper, to taste

Put a frying pan/skillet over a medium heat and add the oil. Once warmed, add the breadcrumbs, lemon zest and garlic and toss together. Fry until golden. Cool slightly and then add the parsley. Season to taste and store in an airtight container.

PASTA SECRET NO.1
how to build a quick pasta

1. PICK A PASTA.

2. PICK YOUR FLAVOUR BASE.
IS IT JUST A LITTLE SLICED OR CRUSHED GARLIC? OR NONE?

3. PICK 2–4 BASE INGREDIENTS.
BACON AND TOMATO, GORGONZOLA AND MASCARPONE? CHILLI/CHILE AND ALMONDS?

4. OLIVE OIL OR BUTTER?
OR BOTH?

5. PICK SOME COMPLEMENTING AROMATICS.
LEMON ZEST, CHOPPED SUNDRIED TOMATOES, KIMCHI?

6. LEAVES, HERBS AND SPICES FOR FLAVOUR?

7. HOW ABOUT A SPLASH OR DASH?
SOY SAUCE, HOT SAUCE, LEMON JUICE, WHITE WINE?

8. TOPPER...
JUST CHEESE AND BLACK PEPPER, CREAMY RICOTTA OR FRIED EGG?

* SEASON TO TASTE.

1. PASTA TYPE AND SHAPE (CARRIER FOR FLAVOURS)

Fresh or **dried**
Whole-wheat or durum wheat/semolina or **non-wheat pasta alternative:** quinoa, buckwheat, corn, barley, rice, chickpea, lentil or spiralized vegetables such as courgette/zucchini or butternut squash
Long, thin shapes for oil-based sauces or small to trap meaty sauces

2. FLAVOUR BASE (WHAT DO YOU FEEL LIKE?)

Garlic, onion, shallots, leek, **anchovy fillets**, soffritto (carrot, celery, onion, garlic)

3. BASE INGREDIENTS (STORE CUPBOARD OR SUPERMARKET)

Cured meats: bacon, pancetta, prosciutto di Parma, cooked ham, sausage, salame, mortadella, bresaola
Smoked/canned/cooked fish: smoked salmon, tuna, sardines, cooked prawns/shrimp, bottarga, mojama, caviar
Cheese and dairy: mascarpone, mozzarella, fresh ricotta, ricotta salata, blue cheese, Parmigiano Reggiano, pecorino, goat's cheese, double/heavy cream
Quick and easy vegetables: canned chopped tomatoes, **fresh cherry tomatoes**, frozen peas, asparagus, sun blush tomatoes, mushrooms, roasted (bell) peppers (jarred), prepped stir-fry vegetable bags, sugar snaps, green/French beans, diced avocado, broccoli, courgette/zucchini, squash

I have put together what I hope is a useful pasta pyramid to easily inspire you with quick recipe solutions. It is intended as a useful prompt for ideas, rather than an exhaustive list. It is a flavour-packed word search! In bold below is an example of a quick-build pasta that I make regularly. Happy searching!

4. SAUCE BASE (KEEPING IT SMOOTH)

The rule here is: oil for oil-based sauces and butter for cheese- and cream-based sauces. Some recipes you use both. In a carbonara, egg yolks are used with hot pasta off the heat to provide creaminess.

oil, butter, egg yolk

5. AROMATICS (FOR MAGIC)

Sundried tomatoes, **lemon zest**, **fresh chilli/chile**, olives (green and black), capers, anchovy fillets, fresh truffles, truffle oil, (dark) raisins, tapenade (green and black), soy sauce, peanut butter, curry paste, fish sauce (nam pla), chilli/chili oil, harissa, miso, kimchi, stock cubes, Marmite, chilli/chili paste, sundried tomato paste, shrimp paste, anchovy paste, pesto (red and green), tomato purée/paste, tomato ketchup, good store-bought pasta sauce (plain marinara)

6. LEAVES, HERBS AND SPICES (TORN, SNIPPED OR SPRINKLED)

Leaves: kale, cavolo nero, spinach, rocket/arugula, baby spinach, wild garlic, watercress

Fresh herbs: basil, **flat leaf parsley**, mint, dill, thyme, oregano, sage, rosemary, chives, coriander/cilantro

Spices and dried herbs: **dried chilli flakes/ *hot red pepper flakes***, chilli/chili powder, cumin, saffron, smoked paprika, dried oregano, freeze-dried parsley, freeze-dried basil, garlic powder, five-spice, curry powder

7. LIQUID FLAVOUR (SPLASH OR DASH OF)

Alcohol: White wine, red wine, marsala, brandy, vermouth

Sauces: soy sauce, fish sauce (nam pla), Worcestershire sauce, Tabasco, lemon juice

8. TOPPERS (FOR TEXTURE AND/OR ADDITIONAL PROTEIN OR FLAVOUR)

Chopped herbs, **grated cheese**, fried or poached egg, toasted nuts, pine nuts, seeds, Greek-style yogurt, tapenade, pesto, torn leaves, torn herbs, crumbled cheese, fried minced/ground beef, bacon bits, crispy prosciutto, mojama, bottarga, caviar, sesame seeds, pumpkin seeds, pangrattato (toasted breadcrumbs), dried seaweed, furikake sesame seasoning, ricotta, mozzarella

***SEASONING (TO TASTE)**

Season your sauce to taste with these ingredients during and after cooking.

Salt, freshly ground black pepper, sugar, honey

WHEN IS IT WRONG TO ADD PARMIGIANO?

Officially tradition says it should not be added to fish or shellfish pastas and risottos, although some do. My motto is live and let live. I personally use Parmigiano with smoked or dried fish like anchovies but not on fresh fish and seafood.

2 PASTA SECRET NO.2
how to cook pasta like an Italian

WHAT YOU NEED FOR BOILING PASTA

1 large pot with a lid, 4–5 litre/quart capacity
1 large colander
rock salt

I rarely recommend investing in specialist kitchen equipment, but when it comes to pasta pots I really believe it is one of the best investments a home cook can make. Proper pasta pots have a 4–5 litre/quart capacity, a large in-built colander and a lid. I have had mine for years and use it for everything from chicken soup and stocks to boiling vegetables.

This ingenious invention is a safe and easy way to drain pasta without rushing to the sink, you simply pull the in-built colander up and the magical starchy cooking water, that is the 'numero uno' pasta secret, stays in the pot rather than being poured down the sink. When purchasing, be sure to look for a minimum capacity of 4 litres/quarts and a large and spacious colander, otherwise no matter the size of the pot your pasta will be confined anyway, which kind of defeats the object.

BOILING PASTA ITALIAN-STYLE

Fill a large pan with water, cover and bring to the boil. (Note: The rule is 1 litre/quart water for every 100 g/3½ oz. pasta.)

When at a rolling boil, add 1 tablespoon rock salt (a palmful) and wait for the water to come back up to the boil. (Note: The rule is approximately 10 g/2½ teaspoons rock salt per 1 litre/quart of water.

Taste the water for salt. You want to make sure that it is salty enough to season your pasta and not too salty to spoil it. (Note: There is nothing worse than unseasoned pasta. You can work as hard as you like making a tasty sauce, but if the pasta you add it to tastes bland, and/or overcooked, the result will be disappointing. Aside from the obvious flavour factor, adding salt to the cooking water also encourages the release of starch from the pasta, which is why salting the water properly is another fundamental pasta secret.)

Add the pasta to the salted boiling water and stir with a long carving fork to stop it sticking together. Bring the water back up to the boil, then lower the heat slightly to avoid the pot boiling over and cook as directed on the packet. Only partially cover with a lid to allow some of the steam to escape, as fully covering will cause the pasta to stew. (Note: Stirring is important, especially with long pastas to make sure that each strand is released and not stuck in the bottom of the pot like a witch's broom! Once the pasta is free and swimming there is no need to add oil to stop it sticking – this is a bit of an urban myth – the rolling water will see to that. Oil is sometimes used in commercial kitchens to prevent large quantities of drained par-cooked pasta sticking together.) Test the pasta to make sure it is cooked and drain.

WHAT DOES 'AL DENTE' MEAN?

Italians like to eat their pasta 'al dente', which literally means 'to the tooth' or loosely translated, with a bite. Their view is that pasta is more easily digestible when cooked this way. Some also believe that pasta cooked 'al dente' has a healthier lower GI (glycemic index) than pasta that is cooked until very soft. In order to achieve this perfect cooking status, it is important to know that pasta continues to cook a little once drained, and further in the sauté pan. To avoid overcooking, drain your pasta just before your preferred 'al dente'.

Take note of the cooking time on the packet, but do not use it as gospel and do test pasta throughout the cooking, as I am noticing more and more that (other than the quality Italian brands) most on-pack cooking times are a few minutes off 'al dente', particularly the supermarket own-label brands and non-wheat alternative pastas. I get to just over halfway and then test regularly.

Once drained and dressed, pasta becomes a matter of extreme urgency and it is very important to tuck in the moment it is ready.

HOW MUCH PASTA?

Pasta secca (dry pasta)

100 g/3½ oz. uncooked pasta per person as a one-course meal

70–80 g/2½–3 oz. uncooked pasta per person as an appetizer

50 g/2 oz. uncooked pasta per person when added to soups

Pasta fresca (fresh pasta)

80 g/3 oz. uncooked pasta per person as a one-course meal

60–70 g/2– 2½ oz. uncooked pasta per person as an appetizer

30–40 g/1–1½ oz. uncooked pasta per person when added to soups

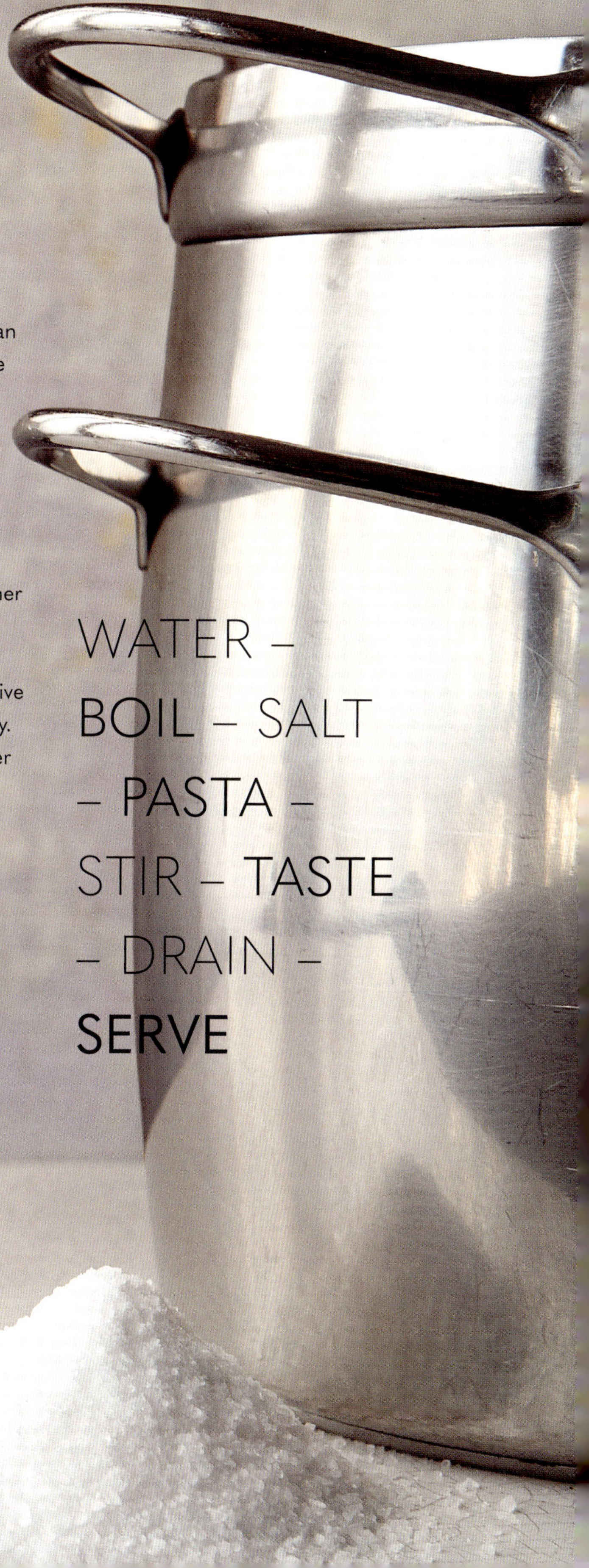

WATER – BOIL – SALT – PASTA – STIR – TASTE – DRAIN – **SERVE**

PASTA SECRET NO.3
'mantecare' – how Italians combine pasta with sauce

WHAT YOU NEED FOR COMBINING PASTA AND SAUCE

1 large sauté pan, wide, deep, heavy-bottomed, long-handled and preferably non-stick
a cup of salty, starchy pasta cooking water (though you might not need all of this)
a glug of olive oil or a good knob/pat of fridge-cold unsalted butter

The act of skilfully combining cooked pasta with a sauce is something we Italians call 'mantecare' or the 'mantecatura'. This literally means to emulsify the starch from the pasta with the oil or butter in the sauce to make that creamy loose pasta finish that is so compelling. It is not an easy thing to do, but once you have it cracked you will never look back. That is why in almost every recipe method I repeat the same words, in the hope that they will become a new mantra in your kitchen: 'Drain the pasta, but keep a cup of the cooking water. Tip the hot drained pasta into the pan containing the sauce, adding a splash of the retained cooking water (about 60 ml/¼ cup) and toss with gusto over a high heat until the pasta looks creamy and well coated.'

Unlike risotto, where only cold unsalted butter and Parmigiano are used for the mantecatura, in pasta, olive oil can also be used instead of butter. This is key for recipes like spaghetti vongole, where the olive oil and starchy water mixed with the garlic, clam juice and white wine create that compelling and super-tasty slippery sauce.

There are two ways Italians combine pasta with sauce:

HOT PASTA INTO HOT SAUCE

Scratch-cook a quick olive oil or butter based sauce in a sauté pan and tip in the hot drained pasta. Add a splash of retained pasta cooking water, if necessary extra butter, and toss with gusto and serve. See Vongole (page 124).

HOT PASTA INTO COLD SAUCE

Place the ingredients in a serving bowl, using raw crushed garlic, a good glug of olive oil and other ingredients of your choice, and tip the hot drained pasta directly into the bowl to unlock the aromatics. Toss with gusto and serve. See Tuna, Rocket/Arugula & Harissa (page 66).

NOTE Cream-based sauces do not follow the mantecare rule, but they often still require a splash of cooking water to loosen the texture. Carbonara is a cross between the two methods above, with the cheese and egg yolks being added off the heat once the hot pasta has been tipped into the pan containing the hot pancetta.

Parmigiano and pecorino cheese are often used as extra emulsifiers in the pan, along with the butter or oil and a splash of the starchy pasta cooking water. This will give you the ultimate in creamy results. A good example of this is Cacio e Pepe (page 49).

WHICH SHAPE, WHICH SAUCE?

Italians have spent centuries developing pasta shapes to catch, trap or elude their saucy counterparts. The general rule is that the long smooth shapes go well with oily sauces (spaghetti, linguine, tagliatelle), where you do not want to trap the oil. Cleverly designed sauce catching shapes and wide fresh pastas go well with hearty meat or tomato-based sauces (shells, rigatoni, fusilli, pappardelle) because they catch all the flavours. Tiny pasta shapes and short-cut fresh pasta for broths and soups. Everything else in-between is all part of the fun; I have really enjoyed exploring and matching all the different shapes, colours and sizes in this book. It is worth noting that each shape, size and type will have a different optimum cooking time.

RED SAUCES 101

All red sauces are equal.

Red sauces may differ in their tomato base, but each red sauce in the Italian kitchen provides a perfect base for seasonal regional cooking. Some make the mistake of believing that fresh tomato sauce is better than sauce made with canned tomatoes. That is simply not true. On a cold winter's day, there is nothing better than the rich deep flavour of slow-cooked canned San Marzanos with a good caramelized soffritto base and earthy oregano. In the same way that nothing can beat raw chopped fresh tomatoes, good olive oil and a generous handful of torn basil on a hot summer's day.

In this section, the big six red sauces are revealed. All delicious, the only big difference is the base tomato used in the recipe:

1. **CANNED/BOTTLED TOMATOES** *Classic Red Sauce*
2. **HEIRLOOM/HERITAGE TOMATOES** *Roasted Tomato Sauce*
3. **CHERRY TOMATOES** *Cooked Fresh Tomato Sauce*
4. **RIPE SUMMER TOMATOES** *Raw Fresh Tomato Sauce*
5. **DRIED TOMATOES** *Sundried Tomato Pesto*
6. **CONCENTRATED TOMATO PURÉE/PASTE** *Romesco*

Today things have changed and we are by and large able to have sweet ripe cherry tomatoes all the year round, and we have grown to eat pesto throughout the year. With that in mind, all I can say is follow your heart rather than the rules made for old seasons that we are sadly losing in some parts of the world. Choose the sauce you feel like eating, match your food with your mood and you will be happy.

1. classic red sauce

Before the days of supermarkets, fresh tomatoes were used for lighter dishes in warmer months. These were then canned and squirreled away for use in the winter. Fresh tomatoes are high in glutamates and bursting with umami, some of which is lost in the preserving process. Italian housewives instinctively added a glutamate-boosting 'soffritto' base and rich tomato purée/paste to their stored summer treasure.

2 tablespoons olive oil
1 Spanish onion, finely chopped
1 carrot, finely diced
1 celery stick, finely diced
2 garlic cloves, finely chopped
1 tablespoon tomato purée/paste1
2 x 400-g/14-oz. cans chopped tomatoes or whole San Marzano tomatoes
a large handful of basil leaves, torn
1 teaspoon sugar
salt and freshly ground black pepper

SERVES 4–6

Heat the oil in a large, heavy-bottomed pan. Add the onion, carrot, celery and garlic and sauté until the onion is glassy and softened. Add the tomato purée/paste and chopped tomatoes. If using whole tomatoes, squash them as they go in to break them up. Add the torn basil leaves and sugar. Season with salt and black pepper to taste.

Cook over a very low heat, stirring frequently to avoid sticking, for 40–60 minutes, or until the soffritto has softened and the sauce is rich, tangy and tasty, and the oil has separated on the surface. I like to leave it chunky, but if you like, you can pass it through a fine sieve/strainer or mouli to remove any chunks and seeds. (*Note:* Do not put it in a food processor as this will change the colour from red to orange.)

2. roasted tomato sauce

This sauce was a late addition to the book, and made because we had so many weird and wonderfully colourful misshapen tomatoes left over from the shoot that it would have been terrible not to use them up. As is often the case it came in last but went straight into my top ten favourites. Fantastic on pasta, but equally delicious on a piece of lightly grilled fish or chicken.

1 kg/2¼ lb. ripe tomatoes (preferably large heirloom/heritage tomatoes)
5 garlic cloves, thinly sliced
1 tablespoon dried oregano
5 sprigs fresh thyme
1 teaspoon raw cane sugar
salt and freshly ground black pepper
125 ml/½ cup olive oil, plus extra if needed

SERVES 4–6

Preheat the oven to 180°C (350°F) Gas 4.

Chop the tomatoes into large chunks, depending on their original size (if cherry tomatoes, just cut in half).

Place in a large roasting tray and sprinkle evenly with the sliced garlic, herbs, sugar, salt and freshly ground black pepper. Drizzle over the olive oil, adding extra if you think it needs it.

Roast in the preheated oven for about 30–40 minutes, until the tomatoes are soft and beginning to caramelize and most of the excess water from them has evaporated.

This sauce can be tossed directly through hot drained pasta or frozen for a later date.

3. cooked cherry tomato

Since we are rarely lucky enough to find sweet sun-ripened tomatoes in the supermarkets, it is important to taste this sauce for acidity when seasoning. As is usually the case, fresh tomatoes are a little acidic, therefore I add a little sugar or honey to sweeten. This does not sweeten the sauce but with the salt and pepper merely removes unwanted acidity and balances the flavours. Taste until you get the balance right.

3 tablespoons olive oil
3 garlic cloves, squashed, peeled and halved lengthways
900 g/2 lb. cherry tomatoes, halved lengthways
a large handful of basil leaves, roughly torn, plus extra to garnish (optional)
1 teaspoon sugar
400–600 g/14–21 oz. dried pasta or 320–480 g/12–18 oz. fresh pasta
salt and freshly ground black pepper

SERVES 4–6

Put a large pan of salted water on to boil for the pasta following the instructions on pages 20–21.

Meanwhile, to make the sauce, heat the olive oil in a large, non-stick frying pan/skillet. Toss in the garlic and cook, stirring, for a few minutes to flavour the oil.

When the garlic begins to colour, add the tomatoes, basil, sugar, and salt and black pepper to taste.

Cook over a high heat for 8–10 minutes until the tomatoes have begun to break down but not totally lost their shape.

When the salted water is at a rolling boil, add the pasta and cook according to the packet instructions.

Drain the pasta, but keep a cup of the cooking water. Tip the hot drained pasta into the hot tomato sauce, add a splash of retained cooking water and toss with gusto over a high heat until the pasta looks creamy and well coated.

Serve immediately, with plenty of extra freshly ground black pepper and fresh basil to garnish, if you like.

TASTY TOPPER *creamy burrata or stracciatella cheese*

SHOWN HERE WITH SPAGHETTINI

4. raw tomato (crudaiola)

This is the quickest sauce in the history of sauces and perfect in the summer months. You can add a little fresh red chilli/chile, if you like. The other beauty of this sauce is all the wonderful things you can add once you have blitzed it, buffalo mozzarella is a delicious addition.

500 g/3 cups sweet cherry tomatoes or sweet ripe juicy summer tomatoes (beef tomatoes, heirloom, San Marzano), the sweeter the better
1 garlic clove, crushed
a handful of basil leaves
5 tablespoons extra virgin olive oil, plus extra for drizzling
50 g/⅔ cup grated Parmigiano Reggiano
400–600 g/14–21 oz. dried pasta or 320–480 g/12–18 oz. fresh pasta
salt and freshly ground black pepper

SERVES 4–6

Put a large pan of salted water on to boil for the pasta following the instructions on pages 20–21.

Meanwhile, to make the sauce, throw the tomatoes, garlic and basil into a food processor or blender and pulse until you get a roughly chopped sauce. Tip into your serving bowl. Stir in the oil and Parmigiano and season to taste.

When the salted water is at a rolling boil, add the pasta and cook according to the packet instructions.

Drain the hot pasta and toss into the raw crudaiola sauce. Mix well and smell the flavours unlock; serve immediately with a drizzle of extra virgin olive oil, and plenty of extra freshly ground black pepper. You can add more Parmigiano if you like, but I do not think it needs it as it masks the delicate raw tomato flavour.

mediterranean variation

ADDITIONAL INGREDIENTS
2 tablespoons olive oil
1 tablespoon capers, drained and rinsed
2 tablespoons black olives, pitted and chopped
2 garlic cloves, thinly sliced
3 anchovy fillets (optional)
a handful of finely diced cherry tomatoes;
extra virgin olive oil
grated Parmigiano, to serve

First, prepare the raw crudaiola as above.

Heat the olive oil in a pan, add the capers, olives, garlic and anchovies (if using), and sizzle until the garlic begins to colour and the anchovies have melted. Add the diced tomatoes, toss for 2 minutes and set aside.

Drain the hot pasta and toss into the pan with the garlic and caper mixture. Add the raw crudaiola sauce.

Mix well to unlock the flavours. Serve immediately with a drizzle of extra virgin olive oil, grated Parmigiano and plenty of extra freshly ground black pepper.

SHOWN HERE WITH
DRIED EGG PASTA PAPPARDELLE

5. sundried tomato pesto

This really simple red pesto recipe can be used on anything from pasta to steamed vegetables, baked chicken or fish.

110 g/1 cup sundried tomatoes, drained
2 garlic cloves, peeled
a handful of basil leaves
a handful of flat leaf parsley leaves
1 tablespoon pine nuts, toasted
½ teaspoon dried chilli flakes/hot red pepper flakes
3 tablespoons grated Parmigiano Reggiano, plus extra to serve
6 tablespoons extra virgin olive oil
200 g/7 oz. dried pasta or 160 g/6 oz. fresh pasta
salt and freshly ground black pepper

SERVES 2

Put a large pan of salted water on to boil for the pasta following the instructions on pages 20–21.

Meanwhile, to make the sauce, place all the ingredients apart from the pasta in a food processor, with just 1 tablespoon of the olive oil and pulse until blended.

Add the rest of the oil, mixing well until you have your desired pesto consistency. Season to taste.

When the salted water is at a rolling boil, add the pasta and cook according to the packet instructions.

Drain the pasta, but keep a cup of the cooking water. Tip the hot drained pasta back into the pan. Add the pesto and a splash of the retained pasta cooking water and toss with gusto over a high heat until the pasta looks creamy and well coated. If necessary, add a splash more olive oil or a tiny extra splash of pasta water to loosen up.

Serve immediately, topped with extra Parmigiano and plenty of extra freshly ground black pepper. This will keep well in the fridge in an airtight container for up to a week.

TASTY TOPPER *shredded rocket/arugula leaves*

SHOWN HERE WITH FRESH TAGLIATELLE

6. romesco

I love this sauce. My favourite use for it does not involve pasta at all. I love to dip baked new potatoes into it... confessions, confessions. Here it is shown with spiralized courgette/zucchini or zoodles, which works really well and is a lot less naughty than my tiny tatties...

3 heaped tablespoons tomato purée/paste
1 large roasted red (bell) pepper, (100 g/3½ oz. from a jar), skin removed*
1 garlic clove, peeled
a handful of flaked/slivered or kibbled almonds, toasted
a handful of flat leaf parsley, finely chopped
1 tablespoon apple cider vinegar
60 ml/¼ cup extra virgin olive oil
1 teaspoon smoked paprika
¼ teaspoon cayenne pepper
¼ teaspoon ground cumin
400 g/14 oz. courgette/zucchini noodles or 400 g/14 oz. dried pasta
salt and freshly ground black pepper
2 heaped tablespoons finely grated Manchego or pecorino, to serve

SERVES 2–4

Place all the ingredients (except the pasta or zoodles and cheese to serve) in a food processor or blender and pulse to a smooth paste. Check the seasoning and set aside.

Cook the zoodles or the pasta (see pages 20–21) according to the packet instructions.

Drain, if needed, and toss the pasta or zoodles with the romesco sauce.

Serve immediately, topped with finely grated Manchego or pecorino and plenty of extra freshly ground black pepper.

TASTY TOPPER *Shredded rocket/arugula leaves*

SHOWN HERE WITH
COURGETTE/ ZUCCHINI NOODLES

BUTTERS, OILS & PASTA WATER 101

The success of these super quick and tasty recipes relies on the holy trinity of pasta cooking: butter or olive oil, salty and starchy pasta cooking water and vigorous tossing. Remember that browned butter should be frothy and golden with a nutty aroma but NOT burnt. Oils should never be browned or burnt. The ultimate butter and pasta mixture is butter and Parmesan, which is not included as a recipe, but I am mentioning it here lest we should forget.

classic browned butter & sage

What's not to like? For a lighter citrus twist, you can add lemon juice to this traditional sage butter.

200 g/7 oz. dried pasta or 160 g/6 oz. fresh pasta
60 g/½ stick butter
8 sage leaves
2 heaped tablespoons finely grated Parmigiano Reggiano, to serve
freshly ground black pepper, to serve

SERVES 2

Start to cook the pasta in plenty of salted boiling water (see pages 20–21) according to the packet instructions.

Meanwhile, heat the butter and sage leaves in a heavy-bottomed pan.

When the butter has melted and begins to colour, but NOT burn, remove from the heat and set aside.

Drain the pasta, but keep a cup of the cooking water. Tip the hot drained pasta into the sage butter, add a splash of cooking water (about 60 ml/¼ cup) and toss with gusto over a high heat until the pasta looks creamy and well coated. Serve immediately with the grated Parmigiano and extra freshly ground black pepper.

TASTY TOPPER *crumbled Amaretti biscuits or crushed toasted hazelnuts*

stock cube browned butter

Don't knock it until you have tried it. Another college favourite and very, very delicious shortcut, even when college is but a very distant memory.

200 g/7 oz. dried pasta or 160 g/6 oz. fresh pasta
60 g/½ stick butter
3 garlic cloves, squashed and peeled (but still whole)
a sprig of rosemary
1 beef or chicken stock cube, crumbled
a splash of white wine
2 heaped tablespoons finely grated Parmigiano Reggiano, to serve
freshly ground black pepper, to serve

SERVES 2

Start to cook the pasta in plenty of salted boiling water (see pages 20–21) according to the packet instructions.

Meanwhile, heat the butter, garlic and rosemary in a heavy-bottomed pan.

When the butter and garlic begin to colour, but NOT burn, remove from the heat and stir in the stock cube. Return to the heat, add a good splash of wine and bubble, stirring, until glossy. Remove from the heat and set aside.

Drain the pasta, but keep a cup of the cooking water. Tip the hot drained pasta into the stock cube butter, add a splash of cooking water (about 60 ml/¼ cup) and toss with gusto over a high heat until the pasta looks creamy and well coated.

Serve immediately with the grated Parmigiano and freshly ground black pepper.

TASTY TOPPER *crispy olive oil fried egg*

umami browned butter

Umami is the ultimate expression of flavour, which can be achieved by melting anchovy fillets into hot butter. You only need a little, but it is truly transformational.

200 g/7 oz. dried pasta or 160 g/6 oz. fresh pasta
60 g/½ stick butter
3 salted anchovy fillets
2 heaped tablespoons finely grated Parmigiano Reggiano, to serve
freshly ground black pepper, to serve

SERVES 2

Start to cook the pasta in plenty of salted boiling water (see pages 20–21) according to the packet instructions.

Meanwhile, melt the butter in a heavy-bottomed pan.

When the butter begins to colour, but NOT burn, remove from the heat, stir in the anchovy fillets and set aside.

Drain the pasta, but keep a cup of the cooking water. Tip the hot drained pasta into the anchovy butter, add a splash of the retained cooking water (about 60 ml/¼ cup) and toss with gusto over a high heat until the pasta looks creamy and well coated.

Serve immediately with the grated Parmigiano and plenty of freshly ground black pepper.

TASTY TOPPER *handful of rocket/arugula leaves*

marmite browned butter

Polarising but perfect. Nothing more to say except I love Marmite. Oh and I think that this recipe originates from the brilliant Anna del Conte, who, as an Italian cook living in England, passed it on to her friend Nigella. I love the work of both these lovely ladies as much as I love Marmite and am paying the recipe forward.

200 g/7 oz. dried pasta or 160 g/6 oz. fresh pasta
60 g/½ stick butter
1 heaped teaspoon Marmite
2 heaped tablespoons finely grated Parmigiano Reggiano, to serve
freshly ground black pepper, to serve

SERVES 2

Start to cook the pasta in plenty of salted boiling water (see pages 20–21) according to the packet instructions.

Meanwhile, melt the butter in a heavy-bottomed pan. When the butter begins to colour, but NOT burn, remove from the heat, stir in the Marmite and set aside.

Drain the pasta, but keep a cup of the cooking water. Tip the hot drained pasta into the Marmite butter, add a splash of the cooking water (about 60 ml/¼ cup) and toss with gusto over a high heat until the pasta looks creamy and well coated.

Serve immediately with the grated Parmigiano and freshly ground black pepper.

TASTY TOPPER *toasted breadcrumbs and/or chopped flat leaf parsley*

al tartufo

I have included this recipe, just in case you ever find yourself clutching a very large truffle and don't have the foggiest idea what to do with it.

200 g/7 oz. dried pasta or 160 g/6 oz. fresh pasta
60 g/½ stick butter
1 teaspoon truffle butter or oil (optional)
50 g/2 oz. fresh truffles (white or black)
salt and freshly ground black pepper
2 heaped tablespoons finely grated Parmigiano Reggiano, to serve (optional)

SERVES 2

Start to cook the pasta in plenty of salted boiling water (see pages 20–21) according to the packet instructions.

Meanwhile, melt the butter and truffle butter or oil, if using, in a heavy-bottomed pan. Once melted, remove from the heat.

Drain the pasta, but keep a cup of the cooking water. Tip the hot drained pasta into the butter, add a little salt and pepper and toss with gusto over a high heat until the pasta looks creamy and well coated. If necessary, add a splash of the retained pasta water to loosen up.

Using a truffle shaver, shave truffle slices over the portions of pasta.

Serve immediately with the finely grated Parmigiano cheese (if using) and plenty of extra freshly ground black pepper.

NOTE Before eating, be sure to mix the truffle into the pasta so it is not only on the top. Mmmmm...

miso browned butter

If there is one thing I shall give my kids when they go off to college, it will be a good brown miso. This pasta is delicious with or without the garlic and is a super quick go-to pasta in my home.

200 g/7 oz. dried pasta or 160 g/6 oz. fresh pasta
60 g/½ stick butter
3 garlic cloves, thinly sliced
2 tablespoons brown miso paste
2 heaped tablespoons finely grated Parmigiano Reggiano, to serve
freshly ground black pepper, to serve

SERVES 2

Start to cook the pasta in plenty of salted boiling water (see pages 20–21) according to the packet instructions.

Meanwhile, heat the butter and garlic slices in a heavy-bottomed pan.

When the butter and garlic begin to colour, but NOT burn, remove from the heat, stir in the miso paste and set aside.

Drain the pasta, but keep a cup of the cooking water. Tip the hot drained pasta into the garlic miso butter, add a splash of the retained cooking water (about 60 ml/¼ cup) and toss with gusto over a high heat until the pasta looks creamy and well coated.

Serve immediately with the grated Parmigiano and freshly ground black pepper.

TASTY TOPPER *toasted sesame seeds*

aglio, olio, pepperoncino

The ultimate post-party pasta or, less sociably, of quick and quiet contemplation.

200 g/7 oz. dried pasta or 160 g/6 oz. fresh pasta
5 tablespoons extra virgin olive oil
1 large whole head of garlic, each clove peeled and sliced along the middle 5 mm/¼ inch thick
6 anchovy fillets (optional)
½–1 teaspoon dried chilli flakes/hot red pepper flakes
salt and freshly ground black pepper
a handful of flat leaf parsley, chopped
grated zest of 1 lemon
2 heaped tablespoons finely grated Parmigiano Reggiano, to serve

SERVES 2

Start to cook the pasta in plenty of salted boiling water (see pages 20–21) according to the packet instructions.

Meanwhile, heat half the olive oil in a large frying pan/skillet. Add the garlic, anchovies, if using, and dried chilli flakes/hot red pepper flakes. Lightly season with salt and plenty of black pepper. Add less salt if using the anchovies, if not using anchovies, season well.

Remove from the heat when the garlic is only just golden on both sides and slightly puffy, and the anchovies have melted.

Drain the pasta but keep a cup of the cooking water. Tip the hot drained pasta into the garlic oil, adding a splash of the pasta cooking water and the rest of the olive oil. Add the parsley and lemon zest and toss with gusto over a high heat, until the pasta is well coated and creamy.

Serve immediately with grated Parmigiano.

bottarga or mojama

Bottarga is salted cured mullet or tuna roe and Mojama (Mosciame) is salted cured tuna loin. Hitherto Mediterranean staples, they are becoming favourites with chefs who use them as powerful flavour toppers.

200 g/7 oz. dried pasta or 160 g/6 oz. fresh pasta
2 tablespoons extra virgin olive oil
2 garlic cloves, squashed, peeled and halved
2 anchovy fillets (optional)
20 g/¾ oz. bottarga or mojama*
30 g/¼ stick butter
grated zest of 1 lemon
a handful of flat leaf parsley, finely chopped
salt and freshly ground black pepper

***If using mojama, omit the anchovies**

SERVES 2

Start to cook the pasta in plenty of salted boiling water (see pages 20–21) according to the packet instructions.

Meanwhile, heat the oil in a large frying pan/skillet. Add the garlic and anchovies. If not using anchovies, lightly season with salt, but take care as bottarga is really salty. Remove from the heat when the garlic begins to take colour.

Drain the pasta, but keep a cup of the cooking water. Tip the hot drained pasta into the oil and garlic, add the bottarga or mojama, butter, lemon zest, parsley and a small splash of the retained pasta cooking water. Toss with gusto over a high heat until the pasta is well coated and creamy.

Serve immediately with plenty of freshly ground black pepper.

QUICK & EASY

Quick and easy...an excellent place to start when you have just got in from work and all you want is food, bath, box set and bed. Most recipes in this section take the same amount of time as the standard 9–11 minutes it takes to cook the pasta. Others take a little longer, but no pasta in this section has a contact time of over 20 minutes for preparing the sauce.

SHOWN HERE WITH ANGEL HAIR PASTA

lemon, mint & caper

Things don't get much quicker than this. Very clean and simple, it almost feels like you just ate a salad...

3 tablespoons extra virgin olive oil, plus extra if needed
a handful of mint leaves, roughly chopped
grated zest and freshly squeezed juice of ½ lemon
1 tablespoon capers, drained and rinsed
2 tablespoons pine nuts, preferably toasted
200 g/7 oz. dried pasta or 160 g/6 oz. fresh pasta
salt and freshly ground black pepper
2 tablespoons finely grated Parmigiano Reggiano, to serve

SERVES 2

Put a large pan of salted water on to boil for the pasta following the instructions on pages 20–21.

Meanwhile, place the olive oil, chopped mint, lemon zest and juice, capers and pine nuts in the bottom of your serving bowl.

When the salted water is at a rolling boil, add the pasta and cook according to the instructions on the packet.

Drain the pasta but keep a cup of the cooking water. Tip the hot drained pasta into the lemon caper mixture, and toss with gusto until the pasta looks creamy and well coated. If the pasta looks too dry, you can add a little more olive oil or a tiny splash of the retained pasta water and mix well.

Season to taste and serve immediately with the grated Parmigiano Reggiano and extra freshly ground black pepper.

TASTY TOPPER *toasted flaked almonds*

cacio e pepe

Cacio e pepe is a famous dish from Rome and literally means cheese and pepper. It is traditionally made with pecorino, but I sometimes like to use a mixture of pecorino and Parmigiano.

200 g/7 oz. dried pasta or 160 g/6 oz. fresh pasta
80 g/¾ stick butter
2 teaspoons freshly ground black pepper, plus extra to serve
100 g/1½ cups grated pecorino Romano, Parmigiano Reggiano or a mix of both

SERVES 2

SHOWN HERE WITH PICI PASTA

Put a large pan of salted water on to boil following the instructions on pages 20–21.

When the salted water is at a rolling boil, add the pasta and cook according to the instructions on the packet, but keep it slightly more al dente than you would like.

Drain, but reserve the cooking water.

Put the butter and pepper in a frying pan/skillet, along with 4 tablespoons of the hot pasta water. Add the hot drained spaghetti and sauté over a high heat for a few moments until most of the pasta water has evaporated. Add most of the cheese and give it all one final toss to combine.

Divide the spaghetti between two bowls and finish by scattering with the remaining cheese and another generous grinding of pepper.

snipped herbs & chilli/chile

This recipe was shared at our first meeting to discuss this book, and remains the perfect example of how quick and easy pasta recipes can be. You can use anything you have in the fridge or make it special by adding tarragon, flat leaf parsley, mint, basil and chives. Thank you, Julia.

4 tablespoons extra virgin olive oil, plus extra if needed
2 garlic cloves, squashed, peeled and halved lengthways
2 generous handfuls of mixed fresh herbs, roughly chopped
½ fresh chilli/chile, thinly sliced, or ½ teaspoon dried chilli flakes/hot red pepper flakes
grated zest of 1 lemon
200 g/7 oz. dried pasta or 160 g/6 oz. fresh pasta
salt and freshly ground black pepper
Parmigiano Reggiano shavings, to serve

SERVES 2

Put a large pan of salted water on to boil for the pasta following the instructions on pages 20–21.

Meanwhile, place the olive oil, garlic, herbs, chilli/chile and lemon zest in the bottom of your serving bowl.

When the salted water is at a rolling boil, add the pasta and cook according to the instructions on the packet.

Drain the pasta but keep a cup of the cooking water. Tip the hot drained pasta into the herb and oil mixture. Toss with gusto until the pasta looks well coated. If the pasta looks a little dry, you can add a little more olive oil or a tiny splash of the retained pasta water and mix well.

Season to taste and serve immediately with Parmigiano shavings and extra freshly ground black pepper.

SHOWN HERE WITH DRIED EGG TAGLIATELLE

raw avocado carbonara

You can make this totally vegan by omitting the egg and the cheese. If you do so, try topping with nutritional yeast instead of Parmigiano cheese, you will be surprised at how cheesy it tastes!

1 ripe Hass avocado, halved, stoned/pitted and peeled
½–1 garlic clove (to taste)
freshly squeezed juice of ½ lemon
a handful of basil leaves
1 tablespoon extra virgin olive oil
2 very fresh egg yolks
200 g/7 oz. dried pasta or 160 g/6 oz. fresh pasta
salt and freshly ground black pepper
2 tablespoons finely grated Parmigiano Reggiano, to serve

SERVES 2

Put a large pan of salted water on to boil for the pasta following the instructions on pages 20–21.

Meanwhile, to make the sauce, place the flesh from the avocado in a food processor or blender with the garlic, lemon juice, basil and olive oil and blend until smooth. Alternatively, use a stick blender.

Remove from the blender and fold in the egg yolks until combined. Season with salt and black pepper and set aside. (Note: If you blend the egg yolks with the avocado instead of folding them in, the mixture quickly becomes avocado mayonnaise – also delicious, but for another time.)

When the salted water is at a rolling boil, add the pasta and cook according to the instructions on the packet.

Drain the pasta, but keep a cup of the cooking water. Tip the hot drained pasta back into the empty pan and add the avocado mixture. Add a very tiny splash of the retained pasta water. Toss with gusto off the heat until the pasta looks well coated and creamy.

Season to taste and serve immediately with the grated Parmigiano and extra freshly ground black pepper.

TASTY TOPPER *toasted mixed seeds*

tomato & mascarpone

I usually make large pots of Classic Red Sauce (see page 25) and keep them in batches in the freezer. Having these on stand-by makes this recipe super quick and easy. Alternatively, you can use a good store-bought sauce and mix with mascarpone. Very yummy.

200 ml/generous ¾ cup Classic Red Sauce (see page 25) or good store-bought sauce
3 heaped tablespoons mascarpone
200 g/7 oz. dried pasta or 160 g/6 oz. fresh pasta
salt and freshly ground black pepper
2 tablespoons finely grated Parmigiano Reggiano, to serve
fresh basil leaves (optional), to garnish

SERVES 2

Put a large pan of salted water on to boil for the pasta following the instructions on pages 20–21.

Meanwhile, heat the red sauce in a pan. When hot, add the mascarpone and heat through until thick and creamy. Adjust the seasoning if necessary and remove from the heat.

When the salted water is at a rolling boil, add the pasta and cook according to the instructions on the packet.

Drain the pasta but keep a cup of the cooking water. Tip the hot drained pasta into the creamy tomato sauce. Toss with gusto over a high heat for a minute or two until the pasta is creamy and well coated. If you need to, you can add a splash of the cooking water to loosen things up.

Season to taste and serve with the grated Parmigiano and fresh basil to garnish, if you like.

SHOWN HERE WITH FUSILONI PASTA

carbonara

It is hardly surprising that out of the top ten classic pasta sauces of all time over half are packed with umami. This creamy Parmigiano and pancetta combination is a worldwide favourite. Don't worry if you don't eat meat or pork, there is an equally delicious smoked salmon version in the fish section (see page 132).

5 very fresh egg yolks
4 tablespoons grated Parmigiano Reggiano
1 tablespoon olive oil
75 g/2½ oz. pancetta, cut into strips
200 g/7 oz. dried pasta or 160 g/6 oz. fresh pasta
freshly ground black pepper
a handful of flat leaf parsley, finely chopped, to garnish

SERVES 2

SHOWN HERE WITH SPAGHETTI

Mix the egg yolks and Parmigiano together in a mixing bowl, season with a good grinding of black pepper and set aside.

Put a large pan of salted water on to boil for the pasta following the instructions on pages 20–21.

Meanwhile, heat the olive oil and pancetta in a frying pan/skillet and fry until the pancetta is browned but not too crispy.

When the salted water is at a rolling boil, add the pasta and cook according to the instructions on the packet.

Drain the pasta, but keep a cup of the cooking water. Tip the hot drained pasta into the egg yolks, mix well and then tip the egg-coated pasta into the fried pancetta. Add a splash of the cooking water (about 60 ml/¼ cup) and toss with gusto off the heat until the pasta looks creamy and well coated.

Serve immediately with a sprinkling of chopped parsley to garnish.

NOTE for egg-based sauces such as this, it is important to add the eggs and toss off the heat, otherwise your eggs will scramble.

gorgonzola & walnut

This sophisticated sauce can literally be knocked up in minutes, particularly if you have toasted the walnuts in advance. You can get an impressive supper party on the table in under 20 minutes with this baby, a good bottle of red wine and a bag of prewashed salad.

150 g/1⅓ cups crumbled Gorgonzola
70 g/⅓ cup mascarpone
100 ml/⅓ cup double/heavy cream
a pinch of nutmeg
200 g/7 oz. dried pasta or 160 g/6 oz. fresh pasta
a handful of walnuts, toasted and roughly chopped
freshly ground black pepper
2 tablespoons finely grated Parmigiano Reggiano, to serve

SERVES 2

Put a large pan of salted water on to boil for the pasta following the instructions on pages 20–21.

Meanwhile, to make the sauce, heat the Gorgonzola and mascarpone together in a pan on a low heat until melted, stirring gently. When they have melted, add the cream and nutmeg, and continue to heat through on a low heat until rich and thick enough to coat the back of the spoon. Remove from the heat and set aside.

When the salted water is at a rolling boil, add the pasta and cook according to the instructions on the packet.

Drain the pasta, but keep a cup of the cooking water. Tip the hot drained pasta into the sauce, add half of the walnuts and toss with gusto over a high heat until the pasta looks creamy and well coated. If you need to, you can add a splash of the retained cooking water to loosen things up.

Serve immediately with plenty of black pepper, the remaining toasted walnuts and the grated Parmigiano.

SHOWN HERE WITH PACCHERI PASTA

ricotta, green olive & basil

When is cream not cream? When it's ricotta. I love the creaminess of the ricotta, combined with moreish olives, fragrant basil and zesty lemon. Again, this feels indulgent but clean. I like to add a couple of handfuls of peppery watercress to this recipe, but it also works perfectly on its own.

2 tablespoons extra virgin olive oil
150 g/⅔ cup ricotta
2 tablespoons green olives, pitted and roughly chopped
a handful of basil leaves, torn
grated zest of 2 lemons
200 g/7 oz. dried pasta or 160 g/6 oz. fresh pasta
salt and freshly ground black pepper

SERVES 2

Put a large pan of salted water on to boil for the pasta following the instructions on pages 20–21.

Meanwhile, to make the sauce, combine all the ingredients apart from the pasta in a serving bowl. Season with a little salt (as olives are salty) and a generous amount of black pepper.

When the salted water is at a rolling boil, add the pasta and cook according to the instructions on the packet.

Drain the pasta, but keep a cup of the cooking water. Tip the hot drained pasta into the bowl. Toss with gusto until the pasta looks creamy and well coated. If you need to, you can add a splash of the retained cooking water to loosen things up. Serve immediately.

TASTY TOPPER *crispy prosciutto*

smoked mackerel & pink pepper

I came up with this warm salad by accident, but the flavours are meant to be.

2 teaspoons pink peppercorns
a handful of flat leaf parsley, finely chopped
½ teaspoon sea salt flakes
¼ teaspoon freshly ground black pepper
4 tablespoons extra virgin olive oil, plus extra if needed
freshly squeezed juice of ½ lemon
200 g/7 oz. smoked mackerel fillets, flaked into chunks
1 large fennel bulb, thinly sliced
1 orange, zested, peeled and segmented
a handful of dill, roughly chopped
200 g/7 oz. dried pasta or 160 g/6 oz. fresh pasta

SERVES 2

Grind the pink peppercorns, parsley, salt, black pepper and oil in a pestle and mortar until the peppercorns are crushed. Add the lemon juice to make a loose pesto-like dressing. Set aside for a moment.

Put a large pan of salted water on to boil for the pasta following the instructions on pages 20–21.

Meanwhile, place the mackerel pieces in a serving dish. Add the peppercorn dressing mixture, fennel, orange zest and segments and dill.

When the salted water is at a rolling boil, add the pasta and cook according to the instructions on the packet.

Drain the pasta, but keep a cup of the cooking water. Tip the hot drained pasta into the mackerel mixture, add a small splash of the retained pasta water and a little more olive oil if necessary. Toss with gusto until the pasta looks well coated and creamy.

Season to taste and serve immediately.

TASTY TOPPER *finely chopped red onion*

pink wink

My Italian cousin introduced me to this delicacy. I had no idea of the ingredients when I was eating it, all I knew was that it was absolutely delicious and very good looking. The trick is to go easy on the ketchup and balance the sweetness with a little salt and plenty of grated Parmigiano to serve. I know this reads like stuff of frat houses and dingy digs, but do give it a try, you might suddenly be serving it at sophisticated dinner parties. I won't tell if you don't...

100 ml/⅓ cup double/heavy cream
2 tablespoons tomato ketchup
a splash of Worcestershire sauce
a splash of Tabasco
200 g/7 oz. dried pasta or 160 g/6 oz. fresh pasta
salt and freshly ground black pepper
2 tablespoons finely grated Parmigiano Reggiano, to serve

SERVES 2

SHOWN HERE WITH CAVATAPPI PASTA

Put a large pan of salted water on to boil for the pasta following the instructions on pages 20–21.

Meanwhile, to make the sauce, heat the cream and ketchup in a heavy-bottomed pan until well combined and beginning to thicken and bubble. Remove from the heat and season with a pinch of salt and black pepper. Blend the cream and ketchup in a food processor or blender with the Worcestershire sauce and Tabasco until smooth, then transfer back into the pan. Alternatively, use a stick blender.

When the salted water is at a rolling boil, add the pasta and cook according to the instructions on the packet.

Drain the pasta, but keep a cup of the cooking water. Tip the hot drained pasta into the creamy ketchup mixture. Add a small splash of the retained pasta water and toss with gusto over a high heat until the pasta looks creamy and well coated in sauce.

Season to taste and serve immediately with the grated Parmigiano and extra freshly ground black pepper.

TASTY TOPPER *well-seasoned flash-fried minced/ground beef – for that deconstructed cheeseburger appeal.*

tuna, rocket/arugula & harissa

Harissa is one of my store cupboard pleasures. I also make this recipe with drained hot brown rice instead of pasta.

4 tablespoons extra virgin olive oil, plus extra to serve (if needed)
1 medium red onion, finely chopped
2 garlic cloves, squashed, peeled and halved lengthways
1–2 heaped teaspoons harissa or chilli/chile paste
grated zest and freshly squeezed juice of 1 lemon
330 g/2 cups cherry tomatoes, quartered
a handful of mint leaves, finely chopped
a handful of parsley, finely chopped
a handful of rocket/arugula leaves, torn
160-g/6-oz. can or jar of tuna in olive oil, drained
300 g/10½ oz. dried short pasta shapes or 240 g/9 oz. fresh short pasta shapes
salt and freshly ground black pepper

SERVES 2–4

Put a large pan of salted water on to boil for the pasta following the instructions on pages 20–21.

Meanwhile, place all the ingredients apart from the pasta in a large bowl. (If you plan to serve this cold, don't add the rocket/arugula at this stage.)

When the salted water is at a rolling boil, add the pasta and cook according to the instructions on the packet.

Drain the pasta, but keep a cup of the cooking water. Tip the hot drained pasta into the bowl of other ingredients. Season with salt and black pepper and toss with gusto until the heat from the pasta unlocks the flavours of all the aromatics. If necessary, add a splash of the retained pasta cooking water or a splash more olive oil to loosen up.

Either serve immediately or allow to cool and store in the fridge to serve later. If you do store it in the fridge, do not add the rocket/arugula until the last minute and remember to remove from the fridge a few minutes before serving to loosen up the oil. Add a little extra seasoning if needed and serve.

SHOWN HERE WITH CHICKPEA CASARECCE

tomato, mozzarella & basil

You can't get an easier pasta salad than this – you don't even have to cook the sauce! When the hot pasta hits all the raw ingredients, it combines all the flavours and unlocks the secrets of these wonderful aromatics. I also make this without mozzarella, replacing it with some chopped anchovies or tuna flakes – it then becomes a quick Puttanesca. A good tip is to remove mozzarella from the fridge around 20 minutes before using, as it becomes creamier at room temperature.

SHOWN HERE WITH CONCHIGLIONI (GIANT PASTA SHELLS)

450 g/scant 3 cups cherry or small heirloom tomatoes, cut into quarters
1 garlic clove, squashed, peeled and halved
a large handful of rocket/ arugula leaves
a large handful of basil leaves, torn
a pinch of dried oregano
250 g/9 oz. mozzarella, cut into bite-size cubes
5 tablespoons extra virgin olive oil
200 g/7 oz. dried pasta or 160 g/6 oz. fresh pasta
salt and freshly ground black pepper

SERVES 2

Put a large pan of salted water on to boil for the pasta following the instructions on pages 20–21.

Meanwhile, place all the ingredients apart from the pasta in a large serving bowl and season to taste.

When the salted water is at a rolling boil, add the pasta and cook according to the packet instructions.

Drain the pasta, but keep a cup of the cooking water. Tip the hot drained pasta into the bowl of other ingredients. Toss with gusto to combine. If necessary, add a splash of the retained pasta cooking water to loosen up.

Check the seasoning and serve immediately.

limone

A popular choice on the terrace at my restaurant Santini during the summer months.

120 g/1 stick butter
finely grated zest of 1 lemon
freshly squeezed juice of 1½ lemons
200 g/7 oz. dried pasta or 160 g/6 oz. fresh pasta
a handful of basil leaves, roughly torn
salt and freshly ground black pepper
crumbled goat's cheese, to serve

SERVES 2

Put a large pan of salted water on to boil for the pasta following the instructions on pages 20–21.

Meanwhile, to make the sauce, heat the butter, lemon zest and lemon juice in a heavy-bottomed pan. When the butter begins to froth, remove the pan from the heat. Do not allow it to burn.

When the salted water is at a rolling boil, add the pasta and cook according to the packet instructions.

Drain the pasta, but keep a cup of the cooking water. Tip the hot drained pasta into the lemony butter, add the torn basil leaves and a splash of the retained cooking water (about 60 ml/¼ cup). Toss with gusto over a high heat until the pasta looks creamy and well coated.

Season to taste, top with crumbled goat's cheese and serve immediately with extra freshly ground black pepper.

TASTY TOPPER *toasted pine nuts*

SHOWN HERE WITH FRESH SPAGHETTI ALLA CHITARRA

SHOWN HERE WITH WHOLE-WHEAT SPAGHETTI

harissa & burrata

A plate where store cupboard meets the sublime. Quickly.

- **2 tablespoons extra virgin olive oil**
- **2 garlic cloves, squashed, peeled and halved lengthways**
- **1–2 tablespoons harissa paste, depending on how hot it is (I use Belazu rose harissa)**
- **200 g/7 oz. dried pasta or 160 g/6 oz. fresh pasta**
- **a handful of fresh mint or rocket/arugula leaves, torn, plus extra to garnish**
- **2 balls of burrata, torn**
- **salt and freshly ground black pepper**

SERVES 2

Put a large pan of salted water on to boil for the pasta following the instructions on pages 20–21.

Meanwhile, to make the sauce, place the olive oil, garlic and harissa in a serving bowl. Season with salt and pepper.

When the salted water is at a rolling boil, add the pasta and cook according to the instructions on the packet.

Drain the pasta, but keep a cup of the cooking water. Tip the hot drained pasta into the harissa mix, add the mint or rocket/arugula and a splash of the retained pasta cooking water if necessary. Toss with gusto until the pasta is well coated with the harissa oil. Gently stir through the torn burrata to create a ripple effect.

Serve immediately with plenty of extra freshly ground black pepper and a few extra mint leaves.

TASTY TOPPER *fried onions, raisins and almonds*

kimchi & bacon

Kimchi is a fermented Korean condiment, packed with umami and heat. An essential metrosexual accessory, but equally important for anyone who loves quick and powerful flavour solutions.

1 tablespoon olive oil
6 rashers/strips smoked streaky/fatty bacon, cut into lardons
2 garlic cloves, squashed and peeled
a splash of wine or sake
60 g/½ stick butter
2 tablespoons kimchi
200 g/7 oz. dried pasta or 160 g/6 oz. fresh pasta
freshly ground black pepper
2 tablespoons finely grated Parmigiano Reggiano, to serve

SERVES 2

Put a large pan of salted water on to boil for the pasta following the instructions on pages 20–21.

Meanwhile, to make the sauce, heat the oil in a pan and fry the bacon and garlic until the bacon is slightly crisp.

Deglaze the bacon pan with the splash of wine or sake, then add the butter and kimchi. Cook until the liquid from the kimchi and the wine have almost evaporated and the butter sauce begins to look creamy and glossy, then remove from the heat.

When the salted water is at a rolling boil, add the pasta and cook according to the instructions on the packet.

Drain the pasta but keep a cup of the cooking water. Tip the hot drained pasta into the bacon and kimchi butter and add a splash of the cooking water. Toss with gusto over a high heat until the pasta looks creamy and well coated.

Serve immediately with plenty of freshly ground black pepper and the Parmigiano cheese.

TASTY TOPPER *olive oil fried egg*

SHOWN HERE WITH ASIAN EGG NOODLES

broccoli & chilli/chile

In Italy, this classic combination is made using the bitter leaves that top turnips (cima di rapa) or broccoli; both work really well.

200 g/7 oz. Tenderstem broccoli
2 tablespoons olive oil
2 garlic cloves, thinly sliced
3 anchovy fillets (optional)
½ teaspoon dried chilli flakes/hot red pepper flakes (optional)
200 g/7 oz. dried pasta or 160 g/6 oz. fresh pasta
1 fresh red chilli/chile, deseeded and thinly sliced
extra virgin olive oil, to drizzle (if needed)
freshly ground black pepper
2 tablespoons shaved Parmigiano Reggiano or salted ricotta, to serve

SERVES 2

SHOWN HERE WITH BLACK BEAN RIGATONCINI PASTA

Blanch the Tenderstem broccoli in a pan of salted boiling water for 1–2 minutes. Drain and refresh under cold water immediately to fix the bright green colour. Pat dry with paper towels and set aside.

Put a large pan of salted water on to boil for the pasta following the instructions on pages 20–21.

Meanwhile, heat the oil, garlic and anchovies in a heavy-bottomed pan. When sizzling, add the broccoli and dried chilli flakes/hot red pepper flakes (if using), turn up the heat and cook until the garlic and broccoli begin to colour. Do not allow them to burn.

When the salted water is at a rolling boil, add the pasta and cook according to the instructions on the packet.

Drain the pasta but keep a cup of the cooking water. Tip the hot drained pasta into the broccoli mixture, add the fresh chilli/chile and a splash of the retained cooking water (about 60 ml/¼ cup) and toss with gusto over a high heat until the pasta looks well coated. If the pasta looks a little dry, add a splash of extra virgin olive oil.

Serve immediately with plenty of freshly ground black pepper and the shaved Parmigiano cheese.

TASTY TOPPER *chopped toasted walnuts*

NOTE you can also add spicy Italian sausage meat to this recipe. Skin a couple of sausages, crumble the meat into pieces and fry off in the pan with the garlic before adding the broccoli. Omit the anchovies if using sausage.

pangrattato & sardine

This is a traditional dish from Southern Italy and is great for getting those beneficial sardines into the system. If you do not like sardines, they can be replaced with a good handful of toasted almonds for a different source of omegas.

4 tablespoons extra virgin olive oil, plus extra if needed
2 garlic cloves, thinly sliced
1 red onion, thinly sliced
1 fresh red chilli/chile, deseeded and thinly sliced
2 anchovy fillets
a handful of (dark) raisins
2 tablespoons black olive pieces, Taggiasche or Kalamata
250 g/1½ cups cherry tomatoes, halved
95 g/3½ oz. boneless sardines in olive oil
½ teaspoon dried chilli flakes/hot red pepper flakes
1 tablespoon pine nuts
a handful of flat leaf parsley, finely chopped
a handful of mint leaves, finely chopped
200 g/7 oz. dried pasta or 160 g/ 6 oz. fresh pasta
salt and freshly ground black pepper
4 tablespoons Pangrattato (page 16), to serve

SERVES 2

Heat 2 tablespoons of the oil in a large, non-stick frying pan/skillet. Toss in the garlic, onion chilli/chile and anchovies and cook, stirring, for a few minutes to flavour the oil. When the onion begins to soften and the garlic begins to colour, add the raisins and olive pieces. Sauté for a couple of minutes before adding the tomatoes. Season with salt and pepper. Cook over a high heat, until the tomatoes have begun to break down but not totally lost their shape.

While the tomatoes are cooking, put a large pan of salted water on to boil for the pasta following the instructions on pages 20–21. When the salted water is at a rolling boil, add the pasta and cook according to the instructions on the packet.

Remove the sauce from the heat and stir in the remaining 2 tablespoons of olive oil, the sardines, dried chilli flakes/hot red pepper flakes, pine nuts and herbs.

Drain the pasta but keep a cup of the cooking water. Tip the hot drained pasta into the sauce and toss with gusto over a high heat until the pasta is well coated. Add an extra splash of olive oil or pasta water if necessary.

Serve immediately with plenty of extra freshly ground black pepper and a sprinkling of pangrattato on each serving.

olive, anchovy & kale

Another of my all-time favourites, these flavours go so well together, it is the stuff of my dreams.

2 tablespoons extra virgin olive oil
4–6 anchovy fillets
2 large handfuls of chopped kale or cavolo nero, tough stems removed
200 g/7 oz. dried pasta or 160 g/6 oz. fresh pasta
2 tablespoons black olive tapenade
freshly ground black pepper
2 tablespoons finely grated Parmigiano Reggiano or aged pecorino, to serve

SERVES 2

SHOWN HERE WITH WHOLE-WHEAT FUSILLI

Put a large pan of salted water on to boil for the pasta following the instructions on pages 20–21.

Meanwhile, heat the olive oil in a large sauté pan. Add the anchovies and kale and season with a good grinding of black pepper. Sauté until the anchovies have melted and the kale has wilted. Remove from the heat.

When the salted water is at a rolling boil, add the pasta and cook according to the instructions on the packet.

Drain the pasta but keep a cup of the cooking water. Tip the hot drained pasta into the anchovy and kale mixture. Add the tapenade and a small splash of the retained pasta cooking water. Toss with gusto over a high heat until the pasta is well coated and creamy.

Serve immediately sprinkled with the grated Parmigiano or aged pecorino cheese.

vodka

Another perfect late night dish. For more vodka flavour, you can add it when the sauce is bubbling and just before you add the peas and remove the pan from the heat. This means that very little of the alcohol burns off and the taste of vodka will be very strong.

30 g/¼ stick butter
80 g/3 oz. cooked ham, cut into bite-size strips
125 ml/½ cup vodka
250 ml/1 cup double/heavy cream
½ tablespoon tomato purée/paste
a handful of frozen peas, defrosted
200 g/7 oz. dried pasta or 160 g/6 oz. fresh pasta
salt and freshly ground black pepper
2 tablespoons finely grated Parmigiano Reggiano, to serve

SERVES 2

Put a large pan of salted water on to boil for the pasta following the instructions on pages 20–21.

Meanwhile, to make the sauce, melt the butter in a large sauté pan. Add the ham and sauté until crispy. Add the vodka, cream and tomato purée/paste. When the mixture begins bubbling, add the peas and remove from the heat. Season to taste.

When the salted water is at a rolling boil, add the pasta and cook according to the instructions on the packet.

Drain the pasta but keep a cup of the cooking water. Tip the hot drained pasta into the creamy sauce. Toss with gusto over a high heat until the pasta is creamy and well coated. If you need to, you can add a splash of the retained cooking water to loosen things up.

Serve immediately with the grated Parmigiano.

SHOWN HERE WITH PENNE LISCE PASTA

one pot pasta

As a traditionalist when it comes to pasta, once again I cannot take credit for this great recipe. This is an adaptation of the iconic Martha Stewart 'one pan' pasta. It is a clever invention indeed, but not one for those who like their pasta 'al dente'.

SHOWN HERE WITH SPAGHETTINI PASTA

350 g/12 oz. dried linguine or spaghettini
350 g/generous 2 cups cherry tomatoes, halved or quartered if large
1 onion, thinly sliced
3 garlic cloves, thinly sliced
¼ teaspoon dried chilli flakes/hot red pepper flakes
4 anchovy fillets (optional, if not using, add an extra teaspoon of salt)
a large handful of basil leaves
2 teaspoons capers, drained and rinsed
2 tablespoons extra virgin olive oil
1 teaspoons salt
a knob/pat of butter
freshly ground black pepper
4 tablespoons finely grated Parmigiano Reggiano, to serve

SERVES 4

Place all the ingredients (except the Parmigiano to serve) in the bottom of a pan that is large enough for the pasta to not be broken.

Add 850 ml/3½ cups water and bring to the boil over a high heat. Stir frequently until the pasta is al dente and the water has almost evaporated (about 9 minutes). Adjust the seasoning to taste and serve immediately with the Parmigiano sprinkled over.

walnut & anchovy pesto

This tasty pesto keeps in the fridge for up to 3 days when covered with a layer of olive oil. It is also delicious on chicken, steaks and fish, not to mention roasted or spiralized vegetables.

a handful of sundried tomato halves, either in oil or dried (dried are more salty, so start with only 3 anchovy fillets)
3–6 anchovy fillets, (to taste)
a handful of walnut halves, toasted until rich and nutty
a large handful of flat leaf parsley
a large handful of basil leaves
a handful of aged pecorino cheese chunks (about 60 g/ 2¼ oz.)
1 garlic clove, peeled
grated zest and freshly squeezed juice of 1 large lemon
100 ml/⅓ cup extra virgin olive oil, plus extra if needed
a pinch of cayenne pepper
400–600 g/14–21 oz. dried pasta or 320–480 g/12–18 oz. fresh pasta
½ bag of baby spinach leaves, washed and spun
400 g/14 oz. Heritage/ Heirloom tomatoes, roughly chopped into chunks
salt and freshly ground black pepper

SERVES 4–6

SHOWN HERE WITH ORECCHIETTE PASTA

Put a large pan of salted water on to boil for the pasta following the instructions on pages 20–21

Meanwhile, place the sundried tomatoes, anchovies, walnut halves, parsley, basil, pecorino, garlic, lemon zest and juice and olive oil in a food processor or blender and pulse to a rough pesto consistency. Add more oil if the mixture is too dry or until you have the desired consistency. Season to taste with cayenne pepper, salt and black pepper.

When the salted water is at a rolling boil, add the pasta and cook according to the instructions on the packet.

Drain the pasta but keep a cup of the cooking water. Toss the hot pasta with enough pesto to coat well. Add the baby spinach leaves and chopped tomatoes and toss again to mix. Add a tiny splash of the retained pasta water to moisten if necessary.

This dish can either be served immediately or prepared a little in advance and served at room temperature.

artichoke, lemon & Parmesan

For those of you familiar with the iconic global dipping sensation, you will know that this artichoke heart, mayo and Parmigiano combination is usually topped with more Parmigiano and baked in the oven. Here I have deconstructed it for a quick and surprisingly good hot pasta. If you don't like the idea of mayonnaise, you can replace it with a good glug of extra virgin olive oil or crème fraîche.

2 heaped tablespoons good-quality mayonnaise
150 g/5½ oz. jarred artichoke hearts, drained and very roughly chopped
2 tablespoons finely grated Parmigiano Reggiano cheese, plus extra to serve
grated zest of ½ lemon
200 g/7 oz. dried pasta or 160 g/6 oz. fresh pasta
salt and freshly ground black pepper

SERVES 2

Put a large pan of salted water on to boil for the pasta following the instructions on pages 20–21.

Meanwhile, to make the sauce, combine all the ingredients apart from the pasta in a cold pan off the heat.

When the salted water is at a rolling boil, add the pasta and cook according to the instructions on the packet.

Drain the pasta, but keep a cup of the cooking water. Tip the hot drained pasta into the artichoke mayo mixture. Add a small splash of the retained pasta water and then toss with gusto over a high heat until the pasta looks creamy and well coated.

Serve immediately with extra grated Parmigiano and extra freshly ground black pepper.

TASTY TOPPER *Pangrattato (page 16)*

SHOWN HERE WITH GREEN LENTIL PENNE

smoked salmon & capers

Who needs a bagel when you have pasta?!

100 g/3½ oz. smoked salmon, cut into bite-size strips
80 g/⅓ cup softened cream cheese or crème fraîche
2 heaped teaspoons capers, drained and rinsed
¼ teaspoon roughly ground black pepper
grated zest of 1 lemon, plus a squeeze of the juice
200 g/7 oz. dried pasta or 160 g/6 oz. fresh pasta
a generous handful of rocket/arugula leaves
salt and freshly ground black pepper

SERVES 2

Put a large pan of salted water on to boil for the pasta following the instructions on pages 20–21.

Meanwhile, to make the sauce, combine all the ingredients in a serving bowl except the pasta and the rocket/arugula.

When the salted water is at a rolling boil, add the pasta and cook according to the instructions on the packet.

Tip the hot drained pasta into the bowl, add the rocket/arugula and toss with gusto until the pasta looks creamy and well coated. If you need to, you can add a splash of the retained cooking water to loosen things up.

Adjust the seasoning to taste and serve immediately.

NOTE you can replace the smoked salmon with strips of prosciutto di Parma for equally delicious results.

SHOWN HERE WITH DRIED TROFIE PASTA

FUNGHI & VEGETABLES

Mushrooms, or Funghi as they call them in Italy, are one of life's wonders. These magical 'sculptures' are packed with umami to make all they touch infinitely more delicious. Vegetables are my favourite food and I eat them every which way. There is something especially healing about 'seasonal' vegetables, they seem to answer the soul's hunger in a unique way. The recipes in this section provide a rainbow of umami-packed and seasonal sauces for throughout the year.

creamy mushroom

This popular recipe forms the basis for many a pasta dish. If you don't fancy cream, you can replace it with Greek-style yogurt or crème fraîche at the pasta tossing stage.

30 g/¼ stick butter
2 tablespoons extra virgin olive oil
2 garlic cloves, finely chopped
350 g/12 oz. mixed mushrooms, cleaned and roughly sliced
½ vegetable stock cube
a handful of flat leaf parsley, finely chopped
150 ml/⅔ cup white wine
150 ml/⅔ cup double/heavy cream
200 g/7 oz. dried pasta or 160 g/6 oz. fresh pasta
salt and freshly ground black pepper
2 tablespoons finely grated Parmigiano Reggiano, to serve

SERVES 2

Heat the butter and oil in a heavy-bottomed pan, add the garlic and sauté until glassy. Add the mushrooms, stock cube and parsley. Season with salt and pepper and sauté until the mushrooms are softened but not mushy.

Meanwhile, put a large pan of salted water on to boil for the pasta following the instructions on pages 20–21.

Deglaze the mushroom pan with the wine. When the wine begins to evaporate, add the cream and heat until bubbling. Check the seasoning and remove from the heat.

When the salted water is at a rolling boil, add the pasta and cook according to the instructions on the packet.

Drain the pasta, but keep a cup of the cooking water. Tip the hot drained pasta into the sauce and toss with gusto over a high heat until the pasta looks creamy and well coated. Add a splash of cooking water to loosen if needed.

Serve immediately with the finely grated Parmigiano cheese and plenty of extra black pepper.

SHOWN HERE WITH
TORTELLINI PASTA

truffled mushroom lasagne

'OMG!' is all I can say about this dish... For an equally good but less heavenly experience, you can swap the pasta for thinly sliced grilled vegetables like courgettes/zucchini or aubergine/eggplant.

8–10 lasagne sheets
100 g/1½ cups grated Parmigiano Reggiano
400 g/scant 2 cups mascarpone

FOR THE FILLING
4 tablespoons olive oil
1 large white onion, finely chopped
3 garlic cloves, finely chopped
a small bunch of thyme, leaves only
1.5 kg/3¼ lb. mixed mushrooms (such as portobello, oyster, shiitake and chestnut/ cremini), cleaned and chopped
125 ml/½ cup white wine
truffle oil, to taste
salt and freshly ground black pepper

FOR THE WHITE SAUCE
40 g/3 tablespoons butter
40 g/generous ¼ cup plain/all-purpose flour
585 ml/2½ cups milk
a pinch of grated nutmeg

25 x 20-cm/10 x 8-inch baking dish

SERVES 6

For the filling, heat the oil in a pan and fry the onion, garlic and thyme until the onion is translucent. Add the chopped mushrooms, season with salt and pepper and sauté until the mushrooms begin to soften.

Deglaze the pan with the white wine, and then cook slowly for 15–20 minutes until all the liquid has been released from the mushrooms and you have a rich, dark mushroom mixture. Remove from the heat, add truffle oil to taste and adjust the seasoning.

Preheat the oven to 180°C (350°F) Gas 4.

To make the white sauce, melt the butter in a heavy-bottomed pan, sprinkle in the flour and stir to combine. When the flour begins to colour, remove the pan from the heat and, using a balloon whisk, whisk in the milk to prevent lumps from forming. Return to a low heat and cook for around 10 minutes until it reaches a boil, whisking constantly so no new lumps form. Remove from the heat, stir in the nutmeg and seasoning then set aside. Once a little cooler, cover the surface with clingfilm/plastic wrap to stop a skin from forming.

Pre-cook the lasagne sheets, if necessary, in boiling salted water according to the packet instructions (or for 3–4 minutes if you have followed the fresh pasta recipe on page 10). Lay them flat on a clean kitchen towel to dry.

Coat the bottom of the baking dish with a ladleful of white sauce and top with a layer of mushroom mixture, a good sprinkling of Parmigiano and six evenly spaced (teaspoon-size) dollops of mascarpone. Top with lasagne sheets (cut to fit if necessary), press down gently and repeat with the remaining ingredients.

When you get to the very top layer of lasagne there is no need to trim the sheets – people love the crispy outer edges that hang over the dish. To stop the lasagne from rising, take a long knife and make several holes reaching right down to the bottom layer – this will create little chimneys of deliciousness! Top with a final layer of white sauce, a few blobs of mascarpone and a sprinkling of Parmigiano.

Cook in the preheated oven for around 40 minutes until the top begins to brown and the lasagne is bubbling.

mushroom ragù

You will start to look forward to meat-free Mondays with this recipe. You can also use it instead of mince in your favourite lasagne recipe, or in my recipe (page 97) instead of the truffled mushroom filling.

3 tablespoons olive oil
1 medium–large Spanish onion, finely chopped
1 carrot, finely diced
1 celery stick, finely diced
5 garlic cloves, 2 finely chopped and 3 thinly sliced
60 g/½ stick butter, plus extra for serving
300 g/10½ oz. portobello mushrooms, chopped into 1-cm/⅜-inch pieces
200 g/7 oz. shiitake mushrooms, chopped into 1-cm/⅜-inch pieces
a sprig of rosemary
1 tablespoon tomato purée/paste
250 ml/1 cup red wine
2 x 400-g/14-oz. cans chopped tomatoes or whole San Marzano tomatoes
a large handful of basil leaves, torn
1 teaspoon sugar
1 tablespoon soy sauce
1 stock cube (vegetable or beef, depending on your preference)
½ tablespoon Worcestershire sauce (optional for vegetarians)*
2 teaspoons mushroom powder (optional but incredible)**
400–600 g/14–21 oz. dried pasta or 320–480 g/12–18 oz. fresh pasta
knob/pat of butter
salt and freshly ground black pepper
4–6 heaped tablespoons finely grated Parmigiano Reggiano or pecorino, to serve

***If not using Worcestershire sauce, you can replace it with more soy sauce or ½ teaspoon Marmite**
****You can replace the mushroom powder with 3 anchovy fillets**

SERVES 4–6

Heat the oil in a large heavy-bottomed pan. Add the onion, carrot, celery and finely chopped garlic (not the sliced garlic) and sauté until the onions are glassy and softened. Add the butter, mushrooms and rosemary and sauté until the mushrooms begin to soften.

Add the tomato purée/paste and deglaze the pan with the red wine. Add the tomatoes, torn basil leaves and sugar. (If using whole San Marzano tomatoes, squash them first to break them up.) Add the soy sauce, stock cube, Worcestershire sauce and mushroom powder. Stir and season with salt and black pepper.

Cook over a very low heat, stirring frequently to avoid sticking, for 1–1½ hours, or until the soffritto has softened and the sauce is thick, rich and tangy. If at any point during cooking it looks like it is drying out too much, add more wine!

Towards the end of cooking time, cook the pasta in plenty of boiling salted water (see pages 20–21) according to the packet instructions.

Drain the pasta, but keep a cup of the cooking water. Tip the hot drained pasta back into the pan. Add the ragù (or a portion of it, depending on how many you are serving) with the butter and a splash of the pasta cooking water. Toss with gusto over a high heat until the pasta looks creamy and well coated. Add a splash more cooking water to loosen if needed.

Serve immediately topped with grated Parmigiano or pecorino cheese and plenty of extra freshly ground black pepper.

SHOWN HERE WITH
PAPPARDELLE PASTA

truffled mac 'n' cheese

I don't know about you but I am not a fan of stodgy, congealed mac 'n' cheese. I believe that the reason a certain big-name packet version is so popular is because it's smooth and loose. This is my sophisticated version of that all-time favourite. You can leave out the truffle oil, if you prefer.

950 ml/scant 4 cups double/ heavy cream
¼ teaspoon freshly grated nutmeg
¼ teaspoon cayenne pepper
1 bay leaf
30 g/¼ stick butter
4 shallots, finely chopped
3 garlic cloves, crushed
1 salted anchovy fillet
500 ml/2 cups white wine
100 g/1½ cups grated Cheddar cheese
100 g/1½ cups grated Gruyère cheese
45 g/⅔ cup grated Parmigiano Reggiano
2 tablespoons black truffle oil
500 g/1 lb. 2 oz. dried pasta tubes or 400 g/ 15 oz. fresh pasta tubes
salt and freshly ground black pepper

TO SERVE
75 g/scant 2 cups toasted Panko breadcrumbs
1 tablespoon finely chopped flat leaf parsley
25 g/⅓ cup grated Parmigiano Reggiano

SERVES 8

In a large heavy-bottomed pan, heat the cream until it is almost boiling, then turn down the heat, add the nutmeg, cayenne pepper and bay leaf and allow to simmer slowly until reduced by half. Set aside.

Melt the butter in a separate pan, then sauté the shallots, garlic and anchovy until the anchovy has melted and the shallots are soft and translucent but not browned. Pour in the white wine and simmer until nearly all of it has evaporated.

Meanwhile, put a large pan of salted water on to boil for the pasta following the instructions on pages 20–21.

Pour the cream mixture into the shallot and wine mixture. Add the cheeses and truffle oil, and season to taste. Set aside.

When the salted water is at a rolling boil, add the pasta and cook according to the instructions on the packet.

Drain the pasta, but keep a cup of the cooking water. Return the pasta to the pan and add just enough truffled sauce to coat the pasta (you want it nice and creamy but not too rich), along with 3–4 tablespoons of the retained pasta cooking water. Return to the heat for 1 minute, and give everything a good mix to make it extra creamy. Pour into a suitable serving dish.

Mix the breadcrumbs, parsley and Parmigiano cheese together and sprinkle over the dish. Serve immediately.

NOTE This recipe makes more sauce than you will need for the pasta, but you can keep the rest in the fridge or freeze it for future use.

SHOWN HERE WITH DITALINI PASTA

creamy beets

I like to keep this sauce smooth and creamy, but if you prefer more bite you can chop the cooked beetroots/beets instead of pulsing.

2 large beetroots/beets, scrubbed, tops and bottoms removed and dried with paper towels
3 large garlic cloves, unpeeled (it needs to be very fresh garlic)
30 g/¼ stick butter
1 tablespoon olive oil
1 Spanish onion, finely chopped
a sprig of thyme, leaves only
1 tablespoon extra-thick balsamic vinegar
a generous splash of white wine
400–600 g/14–21 oz. dried pasta or 320–480 g/12–18 oz. fresh pasta
300 ml/1¾ cups double/heavy cream
salt and freshly ground black pepper
4–6 heaped tablespoons finely grated Parmigiano Reggiano, to serve

SERVES 4–6

SHOWN HERE WITH TRIPOLINE PASTA

Preheat the oven to 180°C (350°F) Gas 4.

Wrap the beetroots/beets in foil, adding the garlic cloves to one parcel. Bake in the preheated oven for around 1½ hours until they are soft enough to easily insert a knife into the centre.

Peel off the outer skin from the cooked beetroots/beets and chop into cubes. Cut into the garlic cloves, scoop out the caramelized centre and set aside with the beetroots/beets.

Heat the butter and oil in a heavy-bottomed pan, add the onion and thyme and season with a little salt and black pepper. Cook until the onion becomes glassy and soft, but not coloured, then add the beetroots/beets and garlic. Season again and sauté for 2–3 minutes.

Meanwhile, put a large pan of salted water on to boil for the pasta following the instructions on pages 20–21.

Deglaze the pan with the balsamic vinegar and a good splash of white wine. Continue to sauté for a further 2 minutes before removing from the heat.

When the salted water is at a rolling boil, cook the pasta according to the packet instructions.

Tip the beet mixture into a food processor and blend until puréed. Return the purée to the pan, add the cream and cook on a low heat until the sauce begins to bubble and thicken.

Taste for seasoning. If you like, add another splash of wine, but if you do, make sure you cook off the alcohol for a minute or so.

Drain the pasta, but keep a cup of the cooking water. Tip the hot drained pasta into the creamy sauce and toss with gusto over a high heat until well coated. If the pasta needs loosening, add a splash of the retained cooking water. Serve immediately with the grated Parmigiano cheese and extra black pepper.

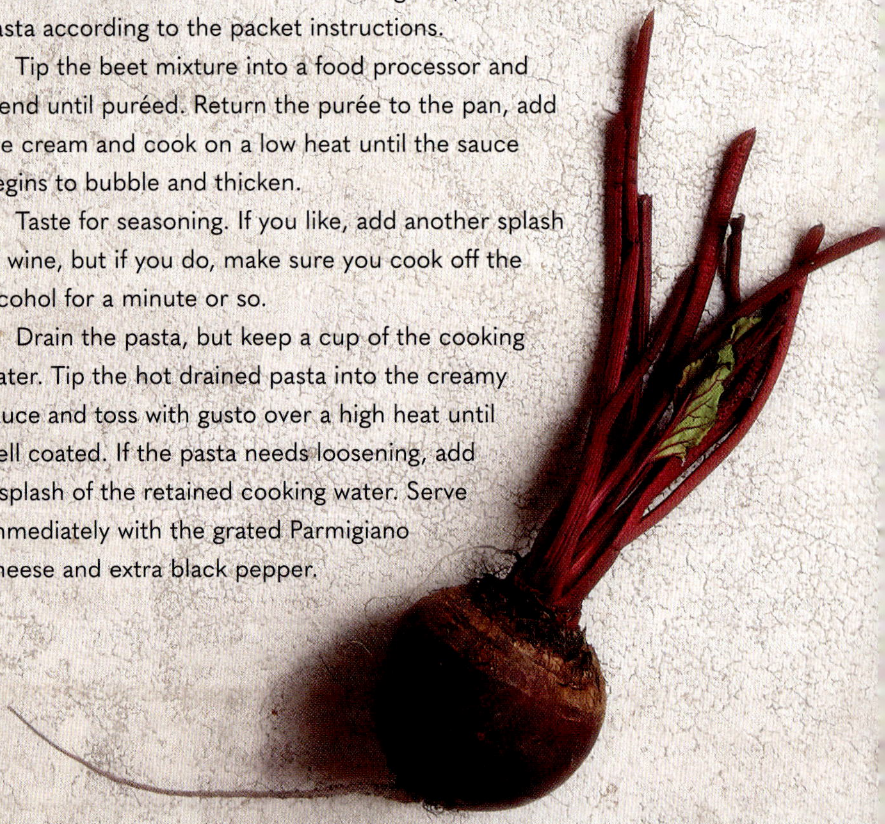

SHOWN HERE WITH
GNOCCHETTI SARDI PASTA

arrabbiata

I first invented this version of one of my favourite dishes in Alassio on the Ligurian coast. New baby, dreamy views and this sweet, tangy pasta, topped with Piemontese ricotta and chewy aubergine/eggplant curls served on big platters, while I was wishing on the watery moon...

extra virgin olive oil
3 garlic cloves, squashed, peeled and halved lengthways
900 g/2 lb. cherry tomatoes, halved
2 fresh red chillies/chiles, deseeded and cut into half moons
½ teaspoon dried chilli flakes/hot red pepper flakes
a large handful of fresh basil leaves, roughly torn, plus extra to serve
1 teaspoon sugar
400–600 g/14–21 oz. dried pasta or 320–480 g/12–18 oz. fresh pasta
salt and freshly ground black pepper
finely grated Parmigiano Reggiano, to serve (optional)

TASTY TOPPER
2 large aubergines/ eggplants
½ tablespoon salt
olive oil
crumbled ricotta

SERVES 4–6

Heat 5 mm/¼ inch oil in a large, non-stick frying pan/skillet. Toss in the garlic and cook, stirring, to flavour the oil. As the garlic begins to colour, add the tomatoes, chillies/chiles, dried chilli flakes/hot red pepper flakes, basil and sugar, and season with salt and black pepper.

Cook over a low heat for 10–15 minutes until the tomatoes have broken down but not totally.

Meanwhile, for the tasty topper, slice the skin from the aubergine/eggplant 1 cm/⅜ inch deep all around. Discard the pulpy core. Cut the skin into 1 cm/⅜ inch wide matchsticks. Place in a colander, sprinkle with the salt and squash with a heavy bowl for 30 minutes.

Drain and rinse the aubergine/eggplant well. Squeeze out all the water with your hands and pat dry with paper towels.

Heat 2.5 cm/1 inch of oil in a pan suitable for shallow-frying (you can check if it is hot with the end of an aubergine/eggplant matchstick to see if it sizzles). Add the aubergine/eggplant matchsticks and fry, stirring, until golden brown and slightly curled. Remove with a slotted spoon and drain on paper towels to absorb any excess oil.

Cook the pasta in plenty of boiling salted water (see pages 20–21) according to the instructions on the packet.

Drain the pasta but keep a cup of the cooking water. Tip the pasta back into the pan, add the spicy cherry tomato sauce and toss with gusto over a high heat until the pasta looks creamy and well coated. Add a splash of the retained cooking water to loosen if needed.

Serve topped with crumbled ricotta, the crispy aubergine/eggplant curls, extra basil and a drizzle of extra virgin olive oil. Serve with extra black pepper and grated Parmigiano cheese if it makes you happy!

squash & sage

Autumn/Fall, on a plate.

½ butternut squash, peeled, deseeded and chopped into 1-cm/ ½-inch cubes
16 sage leaves
olive oil, for drizzling
½ teaspoon dried chilli flakes/hot red pepper flakes
60 g/½ stick butter
freshly squeezed juice of ½ lemon
200 g/7 oz. dried pasta or 160 g/6 oz. fresh pasta
2 tablespoons pumpkin seeds, toasted
70 g/⅓ cup smooth goat's cheese, crumbled
salt and freshly ground black pepper
2 heaped tablespoons finely grated Parmigiano Reggiano, to serve

SERVES 2

Preheat the oven to 180°C (350°F) Gas 4.

Place the squash cubes and eight of the sage leaves on a non-stick baking sheet. Drizzle with olive oil until well coated and season with the dried chilli flakes/hot red pepper flakes, salt and black pepper. Roast in the preheated oven for 20–30 minutes until the squash is softened and beginning to caramelize and the sage leaves are crisp but not burnt.

When the squash has finished cooking, put a large pan of salted water on to boil for the pasta following the instructions on pages 20–21.

Meanwhile, heat the butter, lemon juice and remaining sage leaves in a heavy-bottomed pan. When the butter begins to colour, but not burn, remove the pan from heat. Add the roasted squash (but not the crispy sage leaves) combine, check the seasoning and set aside.

When the salted water is at a rolling boil, add the pasta and cook according to the instructions on the packet.

Drain the pasta, but keep a cup of the cooking water. Tip the hot drained pasta into the squash and butter, add the pumpkin seeds and a splash of the retained cooking water (about 60 ml/ ¼ cup) and toss with gusto over a high heat until the pasta looks creamy and well coated.

Serve immediately topped with the crumbled goat's cheese, the crispy sage leaves and plenty of grated Parmigiano cheese and extra freshly ground black pepper.

SHOWN HERE WITH ORECCHIETTE PASTA

SHOWN HERE WITH
ALPHABET PASTA

sneaky veg pomodoro

For children who don't like to eat vegetables but adore pasta, this is a cunning but loving trick.

3 tablespoons olive oil
1 Spanish onion, finely chopped
1 carrot, finely chopped
1 celery stick, finely chopped
2 garlic cloves, finely chopped
2 tablespoons tomato purée/paste
2 x 400 g/14 oz. cans chopped tomatoes or whole San Marzano
a large handful of basil leaves, torn
1 vegetable stock cube
1 teaspoon sugar
¼ butternut squash, peeled, deseeded and finely chopped
½ large head of broccoli, finely chopped
a handful of peas, defrosted if frozen
2 handfuls of baby spinach leaves, washed
400–600 g/14–21 oz. dried pasta or 320–480 g/12–18 oz. fresh pasta
salt and freshly ground black pepper
butter or extra virgin olive oil and finely grated Parmigiano Reggiano, to serve

SERVES 6–8 CHILDREN

Heat the oil in a large heavy-bottomed pan. Add the onion, carrot, celery and garlic and sauté until the onion is glassy and softened. Add the tomato purée/paste and chopped tomatoes. (If using whole tomatoes, squash them to break them up.) Add the torn basil leaves, stock cube and sugar. Season with salt and black pepper to taste.

Continue to cook the tomato sauce slowly over a very low heat, stirring frequently to avoid sticking, for 40 minutes–1 hour, or until the sauce is rich, tangy and tasty.

Meanwhile, steam or boil the remaining vegetables. To respect the different cooking times, add the squash and broccoli first and then the peas and spinach for only a minute in order to ensure they stay green and vibrant. Drain the vegetables and purée them together (using a stick blender or in a food processor or blender) to a soft paste with a little of their cooking water. Set aside.

When the sauce is nearly ready, cook the pasta in plenty of boiling salted water (see pages 20–21) according to the packet instructions.

Pass the red sauce through a mouli or sieve/strainer and stir in as much of the vegetable purée as you can without giving the game away colour-wise. Adjust the seasoning with a little salt if necessary.

Drain the pasta but keep a cup of the cooking water.

Combine the sauce with the pasta and add a small splash of retained pasta water to loosen, only if necessary. Serve with either a little butter or drizzle of extra virgin olive oil and finely grated Parmigiano cheese. This sauce also freezes really well.

asparagus & peas

If the dish on page 106 was all about Autumn/Fall, this lovely dish is all about Spring, in fact Italians call this combination, Primavera.

60 g/½ stick butter
1 banana shallot, thinly sliced
1 garlic clove, finely chopped
a generous handful of sugar snap peas, trimmed
a bunch of asparagus, woody ends removed and cut into 2.5-cm/1-inch lengths
a handful of frozen peas, defrosted
200 g/7 oz. dried pasta or 160 g/6 oz. fresh pasta
2 tablespoons Parmigiano Reggiano shavings
a handful of mint leaves, finely chopped
salt and freshly ground black pepper

SERVES 2

Put a large pan of salted water on to boil for the pasta following the instructions on pages 20–21.

Meanwhile, melt the butter in a heavy-bottomed pan. Toss in the shallot, garlic, sugar snaps, asparagus and peas and sauté for 2–3 minutes to remove the rawness of the vegetables but still keep them vibrant and relatively crunchy. Season and set aside.

When the salted water is at a rolling boil, add the pasta and cook according to the instructions on the packet.

Drain the pasta, but keep a cup of the cooking water. Tip the hot drained pasta into the buttery vegetables, adding a tiny splash of the retained pasta cooking water. Add the Parmigiano shavings and chopped mint and toss with gusto over a high heat until the pasta is well coated and creamy.

Serve with plenty of extra freshly ground black pepper.

TASTY TOPPER *crispy fried prosciutto di Parma*

SHOWN HERE WITH DRIED EGG GARGANELLI PASTA

classic pesto genovese

This vibrant green sauce captures the flavours of Liguria and is traditionally served with hand-rolled pasta twists called trofie or small linguine called trenette. In Liguria, diced potato and green beans are added to the pasta water towards the end of cooking and drained with the pasta, then toasted pine nuts are scattered on top to serve.

A more delicate and perhaps more 'naïve' pesto can be achieved without the cheese and pine nuts. For a creamy pesto pasta or vegetable dressing, mix equal quantities of pesto with double/heavy cream or mascarpone and heat through gently. For a creamy summer twist, you can mix pesto with Greek-style yogurt or crème fraîche.

2 large handfuls of basil leaves
1–2 garlic cloves, peeled
1–2 tablespoons pine nuts, toasted in a dry pan, plus extra to serve
30 g/scant ½ cup finely grated pecorino
30 g/scant ½ cup finely grate Parmigiano Reggiano
extra virgin olive oil
400 g/14 oz. dried pasta or 320 g/12 oz. fresh pasta
1 large potato, cut into 1-cm/⅜-inch dice
200 g/7 oz. green beans, trimmed and cut into 2.5-cm/1-inch pieces
salt and freshly ground black pepper
2 heaped tablespoons finely grated pecorino or Parmigiano Reggiano, to serve

SERVES 4

Place the basil leaves in a stone mortar together with the garlic, toasted pine nuts and a pinch of salt. Crush the ingredients to release their flavours, taking care not to be rough as this will spoil the texture of the finished pesto. Add the cheeses.

Pour in a fine steady stream of oil, stirring until you reach your chosen consistency (depending on what you are using it for). Adjust the seasoning to taste. Set aside.

Cook the pasta and the potato cubes in plenty of salted boiling water (see pages 20–21) according to the packet instructions. About 3 minutes before draining, add the green beans.

Drain the pasta, potato and beans, but keep a cup of the cooking water. Tip the hot drained pasta, potato and beans back into the pan. Add the pesto and a splash of the retained pasta cooking water. Toss with gusto over a high heat until the pasta looks creamy and well coated. If the pasta needs loosening a little, add a splash more of the cooking water.

Serve immediately, topped with extra toasted pine nuts, grated pecorino or Parmigiano cheese and plenty of ground black pepper.

SHOWN HERE WITH FRESH TROFIE PASTA

feta & spinach

It is usual for pasta dishes to be two-thirds pasta and one-third sauce. This simple salad tips that ratio upside down and instead is two-thirds sauce and one-third pasta. You can apply this upside-down ratio to any pasta you like by adding extra vegetables.

100 g/¾ cup pine nuts, toasted
1 red onion, thinly sliced
225 g/8 oz. feta cheese, cut into cubes
200 g/7 oz. baby spinach leaves, washed
a handful of basil leaves, roughly chopped
100 g/¾ cup (dark) raisins or sultanas/golden raisins
grated zest of 2 lemons, plus the freshly squeezed juice of 1 lemon
about 150 ml/⅔ cup extra virgin olive oil
450 g/1 lb. orzo pasta
salt and freshly ground black pepper

SERVES 4–6

Put a large pan of salted water on to boil for the pasta following the instructions on pages 20–21.

Meanwhile, combine all the ingredients apart from the pasta in a large serving bowl.

When the salted water is at a rolling boil, add the pasta and cook according to the instructions on the packet.

Drain the pasta. Tip the drained pasta into the other ingredients in the serving bowl and toss with gusto until well combined. Taste for seasoning and adjust with salt, black pepper and extra virgin olive oil to taste.

Serve immediately.

NOTE If you would rather serve it cold, do not add the feta or spinach. Allow it to cool and store in the fridge, then add the feta and spinach just before serving, and adjust the seasoning to taste at this stage.

SHOWN HERE WITH ORZO PASTA

sprouts, blue cheese & chestnuts

This dish stands alone in any of the winter months, but really comes into its own around the holidays. Throw in some cold turkey and a handful of dried cranberries to create quick and easy kitchen alchemy at its most powerful.

60 g/½ stick butter
2 tablespoons extra virgin olive oil
2 garlic cloves, squashed, peeled and halved lengthways
350 g/12 oz. Brussels sprouts, peeled and halved lengthways
½ teaspoon dried chilli flakes/hot red pepper flakes
200 g/7 oz. cooked chestnuts, halved
200 g/7 oz. dried pasta or 160 g/6 oz. fresh pasta
150 g/1⅓ cups diced blue cheese
salt and freshly ground black pepper

SERVES 2

SHOWN HERE WITH GIGLI PASTA

Put a large pan of salted water on to boil for the pasta following the instructions on pages 20–21.

Meanwhile, heat the butter and oil in a heavy-bottomed frying pan/skillet, then add the garlic and Brussels sprouts, flat-side down. Season with dried chilli flakes/hot red pepper flakes, salt and black pepper, and cook on a low heat until the flat surfaces begin to caramelize and the sprouts are cooked but not too soft. Add the chestnuts and sauté with the sprouts. Remove from the heat and set aside.

When the salted water is at a rolling boil, add the pasta and cook according to the instructions on the packet.

Drain the pasta, but keep a cup of the cooking water. Tip the hot drained pasta into the sprouts, add the diced blue cheese and toss with gusto over a high heat until the pasta looks well coated. If you need to, you can add a splash of the cooking water to loosen things up.

Serve immediately with plenty of extra black pepper.

TASTY TOPPER *dried cranberries and roughly chopped flat leaf parsley*

Singapore-style

Pasta has no boundaries...

3 tablespoons sunflower oil
4 rashers/strips back bacon, cut into lardons (optional)
150 g/5½ oz. cooked shredded chicken (optional)
3 eggs, lightly beaten
1 onion, thinly sliced
2 garlic cloves, finely chopped
1 fresh red chilli/chile, deseeded and finely chopped
2.5-cm/1-inch piece of root ginger, peeled and grated
1 heaped tablespoon Madras curry powder
⅕ teaspoon Chinese five-spice powder
1 tablespoon soy sauce
1 tablespoon fish sauce (nam pla)
½ tablespoon maple syrup or honey
freshly squeezed juice of ½ lime
1 tablespoon sesame oil
200 g/7 oz. chopped mixed stir fry vegetables
400 g/14 oz. dried pasta or 320 g/12 oz. fresh pasta

SERVES 4

Heat half the sunflower oil in a large, non-stick wok, add the bacon and chicken (if using) and stir-fry until browned. Remove from the wok with a slotted spoon and set aside.

Pour the beaten eggs into the hot oil and scramble; do not make them too dry. Remove from the wok and set aside.

Put a large pan of salted water on to boil for the pasta following the instructions on pages 20–21.

Meanwhile, return the wok to the heat and add the rest of the sunflower oil if necessary. Add the onion, garlic, chilli/chile and ginger and stir-fry until the onion is translucent.

Add the curry powder and five-spice and fry off for a couple of minutes to unlock the spices. Add the soy sauce, fish sauce, maple syrup or honey, lime juice and sesame oil.

Mix well and add the vegetables, then toss until coated but still crunchy and vibrant. Set aside.

When the salted water is at a rolling boil, add the pasta and cook according to the instructions on the packet.

Drain the pasta, but keep a cup of the cooking water. Tip the hot drained pasta into the wok along with the eggs, bacon, chicken and a tiny splash of the retained pasta water, and toss with gusto over a high heat until all the ingredients are well combined and the pasta is well coated.

Serve immediately.

TASTY TOPPER *freshly chopped coriander/cilantro, strips of fresh chilli/chile and freshly squeezed lime juice*

SHOWN HERE WITH SPAGHETTINI

quick pad thai

This recipe is perfect for oodles of rainbow zoodles... or perfect for a quick traditional pad Thai. The dressing is great to keep in the fridge for a quick and surprisingly comforting after work fix. You can choose to use less pasta and supplement with stir-fried vegetables, prawns/shrimp and chicken strips, if you like.

4 tablespoons smooth peanut butter *
3 tablespoons soy sauce
1 garlic clove, crushed
2.5-cm/1-inch piece of root ginger, peeled and grated
1 tablespoon honey
1 tablespoon toasted sesame oil
1 fresh red chilli/chile, deseeded and finely chopped
1 tablespoon apple cider vinegar
1 teaspoon fish sauce (nam pla)
a dash of Tabasco or hot sauce, to taste
freshly squeezed juice of ½ lime
500 g/1 lb. 2 oz dried noodles or 400 g/15 oz. fresh noodles

*** if using unsweetened peanut butter, add more honey to taste.**

SERVES 4–6

Place all the ingredients apart from the noodles in a heavy-bottomed pan and heat on a very low heat until the peanut butter has melted. Stir together gently to combine and remove from the heat immediately. The mixture should never really heat up but just become runny enough to stir the noodles through. Set aside.

Soak the noodles in boiling water according to the instructions on the packet.

Drain the noodles, but keep a cup of the soaking water. Tip the hot drained noodles into the peanut butter dressing, add a splash of the retained soaking water (about 60 ml/¼ cup) and toss with gusto over a high heat until the noodles look creamy and well coated.

Serve immediately.

TASTY TOPPER *roasted cashew nuts or fried diced tofu*

SHOWN HERE WITH RICE NOODLES

FISH & SEAFOOD

There is nothing that evokes the memories of delicious sun-filled holidays more than chilled white wine and a bowl of perfect seafood pasta. This section of the book is designed to allow the recreation of those special memories at home. Some recipes are quicker than others and some molluscs or crustaceans can be as daunting as they are delicious, but the book would not have been complete without the inclusion of these classics. With the help of a good fishmonger, you can master these in moments. The key to the success of these recipes is quality super-fresh ingredients.

vongole

SHOWN HERE WITH BUCKWHEAT SPAGHETTI

Spaghetti vongole has to be high on the top-ten pasta dishes of all time. Served with a chilled Pinot Grigio, it literally tastes like a holiday in a bowl.

700 g/1½ lb. 'vongole' (fresh, live baby clams)*
200 g/7 oz. dried pasta or 160 g/6 oz. fresh pasta
extra virgin olive oil
2 garlic cloves, thinly sliced
1 fresh red chilli/chile, deseeded and thinly sliced
a large handful of flat leaf parsley, finely chopped
125 ml/½ cup white wine
salt and freshly ground black pepper

SERVES 2

Prepare your vongole for cooking (see note). Ensure that you have everything prepped to cook the vongole before you begin to cook the pasta. The pasta cooking time should be timed carefully to coincide with the sauce being ready.

When ready, start to cook the pasta in plenty of boiling salted water (see pages 20–21) according to the packet instructions.

Meanwhile, heat a good glug of olive oil (enough to cover the whole base) in a large pan that has a lid. Add the sliced garlic.

When the garlic begins to colour, turn up the heat and add the clams, chilli/chile and half the parsley. Cover with the lid. Cook for 5–7 minutes, shaking frequently to help the clams open up. Discard any clams that are still closed and splash the others with the white wine.

When the wine has evaporated, add the rest of the chopped parsley and plenty of freshly ground black pepper. As clams are salty by nature, taste the sauce before seasoning further.

Drain the pasta, but keep a cup of the cooking water. Tip the hot drained pasta into the vongole, add a splash of retained cooking water and toss with gusto over a high heat until the pasta looks creamy and well coated.

Serve immediately with plenty of extra ground black pepper.

* **NOTE** Fresh clams should be cleaned well before cooking. Rinse them in several changes of cold water until the water is clear. Then add a handful of sea salt and leave to 'purge' in cold salted water for a few hours. Drain and rinse before using. Discard any shells that are open and do not snap shut when tapped, as they are potentially dangerous.

puttanesca

I could not have a book about pasta, without including slutty spaghetti. In the picture we have used chocolate-/cacao-flavoured pasta, with remarkably satisfying results.

- **3 tablespoons extra virgin olive oil**
- **2 garlic cloves, thinly sliced**
- **1 fresh red chilli/chile, deseeded and finely sliced, or ½ teaspoon dried chilli flakes/hot red pepper flakes**
- **200 g/1¼ cups cherry tomatoes, halved lengthways**
- **2 tablespoons Taggiasche or Kalamata olives, drained, pitted and roughly chopped**
- **2 tablespoons capers, drained and rinsed**
- **3 anchovy fillets**
- **a handful of basil leaves, torn, or flat leaf parsley, roughly chopped (optional)**
- **freshly ground black pepper**
- **200 g/7 oz. dried pasta or 160 g/6 oz. fresh pasta**
- **2 heaped tablespoons finely grated Parmigiano Reggiano, to serve**

SERVES 2

Put a large pan of salted water on to boil for the pasta following the instructions on pages 20–21.

Meanwhile, to make the sauce, heat the olive oil in a heavy-bottomed pan and add the garlic and chilli/chile. When the garlic begins to colour, stir in all the other ingredients apart from the pasta and season with black pepper (the olives, capers and anchovies will probably make it salty enough).

Allow to simmer gently on a low heat for about 8–12 minutes, or until the tomatoes begin to break down. If the tomatoes are too acidic, you can balance them with a pinch of sugar when you adjust the seasoning.

While the sauce is simmering, add the pasta to the boiling water and cook according to the instructions on the packet.

Drain the pasta, but keep a cup of the cooking water. Tip the hot drained pasta into the sauce with a splash of the retained pasta cooking water. Toss with gusto over a high heat until the pasta looks creamy and well coated.

Serve immediately with the Parmigiano cheese and plenty of extra freshly ground black pepper.

SHOWN HERE WITH SPAGHETTI AL CACAO

crab, chilli/chile & lemon

Second to the carbonara, this is the other most popular pasta served at Santini. I think this recipe is loved because it is light, clean, fresh and super tasty.

200 g/7 oz. cooked picked white crabmeat*
a handful of flat leaf parsley, chopped
4 tablespoons extra virgin olive oil, plus extra if needed
grated zest and freshly squeezed juice of 1 lemon
2 garlic cloves, squashed, peeled and halved lengthways
1 fresh red chilli/chile, deseeded and finely chopped
200 g/7 oz. dried pasta or 160 g/6 oz. fresh pasta
salt and freshly ground black pepper

*** You can use half white crabmeat and half brown for a fuller crab flavour.**

SERVES 2

Put a large pan of salted water on to boil for the pasta following the instructions on pages 20–21.

Meanwhile, to make the sauce, combine the remaining ingredients apart from the pasta in a bowl. This is a fairly loose sauce, therefore add extra olive oil if it is too dry, and season with salt and black pepper.

When the salted water is at a rolling boil, add the pasta and cook according to the instructions on the packet.

Drain the pasta, but keep a cup of the cooking water. Tip the hot drained pasta back into the pan, add the crab mixture and a small splash of the retained pasta cooking water. Toss with gusto until creamy and well combined.

Remove the halved garlic cloves and serve immediately.

TASTY TOPPER *diced avocado and mango*

SHOWN HERE WITH LINGUINE

shrimp & chorizo

Bring on the chilled rosé.

4 tablespoons extra virgin olive oil
2 garlic cloves, squashed, peeled and halved lengthways
75 g/3oz. chorizo picante, cut into bite-size rounds
1 fresh red chilli/chile, deseeded and thinly sliced
¼ teaspoon dried chilli flakes/hot red pepper flakes (optional)
200 g/7 oz. dried pasta or 160 g/6 oz. fresh pasta
150 g/5½ oz. raw king prawns/jumbo shrimp, peeled
115 g/1 cup cherry tomatoes, quartered
a handful of basil leaves, torn
grated zest and freshly squeezed juice of 1 lemon
a generous handful of rocket/arugula leaves, torn
salt and freshly ground black pepper

SERVES 2

SHOWN HERE WITH RED LENTIL SPAGHETTI

Put a large pan of salted water on to boil for the pasta following the instructions on pages 20–21.

Meanwhile, to make the sauce, heat 2 tablespoons of the oil in a large, non-stick frying pan/skillet. Add the garlic and cook, stirring, for a few minutes to flavour the oil. When the garlic begins to colour, add the chorizo, chilli/chile and dried chilli flakes/hot red pepper flakes (if using).

When the salted water is at a rolling boil, add the pasta and cook according to the instructions on the packet.

When the chorizo is sizzling, throw in the the prawns/shrimp, tomatoes, basil and lemon juice. Season with salt and black pepper to taste. Cook over a high heat until the prawns/shrimp turn from grey to pink and the tomatoes begin to soften but not disappear. Add the lemon zest, check the seasoning and remove from the heat.

Drain the pasta, but keep a cup of the cooking water. Tip the hot drained pasta into the tomato, prawn/shrimp and chorizo sauce, adding a small splash of the retained pasta cooking water and the remaining olive oil, if necessary. Throw in the rocket/arugula leaves and toss with gusto over a high heat until the pasta is well coated and creamy.

Serve immediately with plenty of extra freshly ground black pepper.

smoked salmon carbonara

Crispy lardons of smoked salmon replace traditional pancetta in this version of an uber-indulgent carbonara.

SHOWN HERE WITH BAVETTE PASTA

3 very fresh egg yolks
50 g/2 oz. salmon caviar (optional)
60 g/½ stick butter
2 anchovy fillets
70–100 g/2½-3½ oz. smoked salmon, chopped into 'lardons' *
200 g/7 oz. dried pasta or 160 g/6 oz. fresh pasta
freshly ground black pepper

***If using salmon caviar, stick to 70 g/2½ oz. salmon.**

SERVES 2

Put a large pan of salted water on to boil for the pasta following the instructions on pages 20–21.

Meanwhile, place the egg yolks in a mixing bowl and mix with the caviar, if using. Season with plenty of black pepper and set aside.

Heat the butter and anchovy fillets in a frying pan/skillet. When the anchovies have melted, add the smoked salmon and fry until crispy. Set aside.

When the salted water is at a rolling boil, add the pasta and cook according to the instructions on the packet.

Drain the pasta, but keep a cup of the cooking water. Tip the hot drained pasta into the egg yolks, mix well and then tip into the salmon and butter mixture. Add a splash of cooking water (about 60 ml/¼ cup) and toss with gusto off the heat until the pasta looks creamy and well coated.

NOTE for egg-based sauces such as this, it is important to add the eggs and toss off the heat, otherwise your eggs will scramble. Serve immediately.

TASTY TOPPER *roughly chopped dill*

SHOWN HERE WITH
TRENETTE PASTA

scoglio

'Scoglio' means rock, but in this context, the word is used to describe rock pools on the seashore – the perfect place for crustaceans of all kinds to live. I like to think of this as 'seashore pasta'.

200 g/7 oz. mussels, purged, scrubbed and beards removed
5 tablespoons extra virgin olive oil
2 garlic cloves, 1 squashed, peeled and halved lengthways and 1 finely chopped
½ handful of flat leaf parsley, chopped
60 ml/¼ cup dry white wine
1 fresh red chilli/chile, deseeded and thinly sliced
3 vine-ripened tomatoes, chopped
1 tablespoon tomato purée/paste
3–4 basil leaves, torn
1 teaspoon sugar (optional)
200 g/7 oz. dried pasta or 160 g/6 oz. fresh pasta
100 g/3½ oz. fresh squid, cleaned and cut in rings
100 g/3½ oz. raw king prawns/jumbo shrimp, peeled
salt and freshly ground black pepper

SERVES 2

Check the mussels by ensuring they are all closed. Discard any open ones. Heat 2 tablespoons of the olive oil in a heavy-bottomed pan and add the halved garlic clove.

When the garlic begins to colour, add the mussels, half the parsley and the white wine. Cover with a lid. The heat will open the mussels. Once the mussels are all open, remove from the heat and leave to cool down. Once cool, retain the mussel stock and set aside. Remove the mussels from their shells and set aside. Discard the shells.

Heat a further tablespoon of oil with the chopped garlic and sliced chilli/chile. When the garlic begins to colour, add the chopped tomatoes, tomato purée/paste, basil leaves and the retained stock from the mussels. You may need to add the teaspoon of sugar if the tomatoes are very acidic to balance the flavours. Simmer uncovered on a low heat for around 10 minutes until the mussels stock has been absorbed and the sauce is no longer too runny.

Meanwhile, start to cook the pasta in plenty of salted boiling water (see pages 20–21) following the instructions on the packet. The pasta cooking should be timed carefully to coincide with the sauce being ready.

When the tomato sauce has been cooking for 10 minutes, add the squid and prawns/shrimp and cook for 3–4 minutes. Season to taste with salt and black pepper, add the mussels and remove from the heat.

Drain the pasta, but keep a cup of the cooking water. Tip the hot drained pasta into the sauce with a splash of the retained pasta cooking water, the final 2 tablespoons of olive oil and the remaining parsley. Toss with gusto over a high heat until the pasta looks creamy and well coated.

Serve immediately with extra ground black pepper.

lobster

Another very popular dish at Santini, this is a pasta that most people choose to order in restaurants rather than cook at home. However, if you buy ready prepared lobster meat from your fishmonger, this dish is actually remarkably easy, and does not involve dealing with a live lobster which can be tricky. There is something very sexy about preparing spaghetti lobster for someone your heart flutters for.

4 tablespoons extra virgin olive oil
1 banana shallot, thinly sliced
2 garlic cloves, thinly sliced
1 fresh red chilli/chile, deseeded and finely chopped
1 large ripe tomato, chopped (San Marzano are the best)
5 basil leaves
125 ml/½ cup white wine
200 g/7 oz. dried pasta or 160 g/6 oz. fresh pasta
300 g/10½ oz. lobster meat, cooked and picked
6 cherry tomatoes, quartered
a handful of flat leaf parsley, finely chopped
salt and freshly ground black pepper

SERVES 2

Put a large pan of salted water on to boil for the pasta following the instructions on pages 20–21.

Meanwhile, to make the sauce, heat 2 tablespoons of the olive oil in a heavy-bottomed pan and add the shallot, garlic and chilli/chile.

When the garlic begins to colour, add the chopped tomato (not the cherry tomatoes), basil leaves and white wine. Season with salt and black pepper and leave to cook until the tomato starts to break down.

When the salted water is at a rolling boil, add the pasta and cook according to the instructions on the packet.

When half of the wine has evaporated and the tomato is soft, add the lobster meat. Heat through quickly (the longer it stays in the pan, the tougher it will become) and then remove from the heat.

Drain the pasta, but keep a cup of the cooking water. Tip the hot drained pasta into the lobster sauce with a splash of the retained pasta cooking water, the cherry tomatoes, parsley and the remaining 2 tablespoons of olive oil. Toss with gusto over a high heat until the pasta looks creamy and well coated.

Serve immediately with plenty of extra freshly ground black pepper.

SHOWN HERE WITH SPAGHETTI

scallop & crispy prosciutto

The key ingredient in this dish is not the scallops or the prosciutto as you might expect, but the tasty seed 'grattato'. This fresh, nutty, garlicky, lemony, cheesy mixture, really does complement the sweet scallops and the umami-packed prosciutto in an extraordinary way.

4 tablespoons extra virgin olive oil
1 garlic clove, squashed, peeled and halved lengthways
6 scallops, preferably with coral, halved if large
200 g/7 oz. dried pasta or 160 g/6 oz. fresh pasta
freshly squeezed juice of 1 lemon
2 slices of Prosciutto di Parma, baked in the oven until crisp, then broken into shards

FOR THE PUMPKIN SEED GRATTATO

2 tablespoons pumpkin seeds, toasted
a handful of flat leaf parsley
grated zest of 2 lemons
2 tablespoons finely grated Parmigiano Reggiano
1 garlic clove, finely chopped
salt and freshly ground black pepper

SERVES 2

Start by making the pumpkin seed grattato. Place the toasted pumpkin seeds, parsley, lemon zest, Parmigiano cheese and garlic in a food processor and pulse until the mixture resembles coarse breadcrumbs. Season with salt and black pepper to taste. Set aside.

Put a large pan of salted water on to boil for the pasta following the instructions on pages 20–21.

Meanwhile, heat 2 tablespoons of the olive oil and the garlic halves in a heavy-bottomed pan. When the garlic begins to colour, add the scallops. Cook on a high heat, turning once, until the scallops are cooked through, about 5 minutes for large scallops.

When the scallops are cooked, season them with salt and pepper and remove from the heat. You want the scallops to be cooked through but not chewy. They should spring back when poked and not be hard to the touch. Set aside.

When the salted water is at a rolling boil, add the pasta and cook according to the instructions on the packet.

Drain the pasta, but keep a cup of the cooking water. Tip the hot drained pasta into the scallops. Add the lemon juice, a splash of the retained pasta cooking water, the pumpkin seed grattato and the rest of the oil. Toss with gusto over a high heat until the pasta looks creamy and well coated.

Serve immediately topped with the crispy Prosciutto di Parma and plenty of extra freshly ground black pepper.

SHOWN HERE WITH
KAMUT SPAGHETTI

'in salsa'

This typically Venetian pasta is served with bigoli, a thick, spaghetti-like pasta with a tiny hole through the centre. I don't have to tell you what a powerful combination the sweet onion and salty, umami-packed anchovies make.

3–4 tablespoons olive oil
2 large onions, thinly sliced
200 g/7 oz. anchovy fillets in olive oil, drained
freshly ground black pepper
400 g/14 oz. dried pasta or 320 g/12 oz. fresh pasta
finely grated Parmigiano Reggiano, to serve

SERVES 4

Put a large pan of salted water on to boil for the pasta following the instructions on pages 20–21.

Meanwhile, to make the sauce, heat the oil in a heavy-bottomed pan. Add the onions and cook until golden. Add the anchovies and black pepper, then stir until the anchovies have dissolved into the softened onions.

When the salted water is at a rolling boil, add the pasta and cook according to the instructions on the packet.

Drain the pasta, but keep a cup of the cooking water. Tip the hot drained pasta into the anchovy and onion sauce, adding a small splash of the retained pasta cooking water. Toss with gusto over a high heat until the pasta is well coated and creamy.

Serve immediately with Parmigiano and plenty of extra freshly ground black pepper.

SHOWN HERE WITH BIGOLI PASTA

shrimp & courgette/zucchini

The addition of a splash of vinegar to courgette/zucchini cooked in this way is called 'al scapece', which is a term that signifies a sort of sweet-and-sour expectation. The sweet vegetables and prawns/shrimp work brilliantly with the drizzle of a syrupy aged balsamic vinegar.

4 tablespoons extra virgin olive oil
2 garlic cloves, squashed, peeled and halved lengthways
150 g/5½ oz. courgettes/ zucchini, sliced into 5-mm/¼-inch discs
a small handful of mint leaves, finely chopped
125 g/4½ oz. raw king prawns/jumbo shrimp, peeled
200 g/7 oz. dried pasta or 160 g/6 oz. fresh pasta
grated zest of 1 lemon
salt and freshly ground black pepper
thick balsamic vinegar or glaze, to drizzle

SERVES 2

SHOWN HERE WITH FRESH TAGLIATELLE PASTA

Put a large pan of salted water on to boil for the pasta following the instructions on pages 20–21.

Meanwhile, heat 2 tablespoons of the oil in a large, non-stick frying pan/skillet. Toss in the garlic and cook, stirring, for a few minutes to flavour the oil.

When the garlic begins to colour, add the courgettes/zucchini and half of the mint and stir fry. When the courgettes/zucchini begin to soften, but are still al dente, add the prawns/shrimp. Cook until the prawns/shrimp turn pink, then season with salt and pepper and toss until the shrimp are cooked but still tender. Remove from the heat.

When the salted water is at a rolling boil, add the pasta and cook according to the instructions on the packet.

Drain the pasta, but keep a cup of the cooking water. Tip the hot drained pasta into the courgette/zucchini and prawn/shrimp mixture, adding a small splash of the retained cooking water, the remaining mint, lemon zest and remaining oil. Toss with gusto over a high heat until the pasta is well coated and creamy.

Serve immediately with a generous drizzle of thick balsamic vinegar or glaze and plenty of extra freshly ground black pepper.

SHOWN HERE WITH TRENETTE PASTA

calamari & 'nduja

'Nduja is a spreadable Calabrian super spicy cured salame. Like bottarga and mojama, 'nduja is one of the new trendy ingredients used by modern chefs and available in speciality stores. It also comes in jars as an ambient product and has a long shelf-life. Italians also spread it on bread. If you keep this unique ingredient in your pantry, it can really make you look good when rustling up that unexpected pasta for guests.

2 tablespoons extra virgin olive oil
2 garlic cloves, squashed, peeled and halved lengthways
200 g/7 oz. dried pasta or 160 g/6 oz. fresh pasta
2–3 tablespoons 'nduja, to taste
300 g/10½ oz. squid, cleaned, washed and cut into rings
a handful of basil leaves, torn, or flat leaf parsley, roughly chopped
a generous handful of rocket/arugula, torn
grated zest of 1 lemon
salt and freshly ground black pepper

SERVES 2

Put a large pan of salted water on to boil for the pasta following the instructions on pages 20–21.

Meanwhile, to make the sauce, heat the oil in a large, non-stick frying pan/skillet. Toss in the garlic and cook, stirring, for a few minutes to flavour the oil.

When the salted water is at a rolling boil, add the pasta and cook according to the instructions on the packet.

When the garlic begins to colour, add 1 tablespoon of the 'nduja and the squid rings. Season and sauté on a high heat for 3–4 minutes until the squid is cooked but not rubbery. Remove from the heat, stir in the rest of the 'nduja paste and the basil leaves or parsley and set aside.

Drain the pasta, but keep a cup of the cooking water. Tip the hot drained pasta into the squid and 'nduja sauce, adding a small splash of the retained pasta cooking water and a little more olive oil if necessary. Add the rocket/arugula and lemon zest and toss with gusto over a high heat until the pasta is well coated and creamy.

Serve immediately with plenty of extra freshly ground black pepper.

fresh tuna ragù

I am a big fan of seared fresh tuna, so I have taken the principles of a classic tuna ragù dish and deconstructed it to my taste. Delicious!

6 tablespoons extra virgin olive oil
2 garlic cloves, 1 finely sliced and 1 squashed, peeled and halved lengthways
4 anchovy fillets or 1 teaspoon anchovy paste
¼ teaspoon dried chilli flakes/hot red pepper flakes
1 onion, thinly sliced
½ tablespoon capers, drained and rinsed
a little squeeze of tomato purée/paste
150 ml/⅔ cup white wine
450 g/scant 3 cups cherry tomatoes, halved
1 fresh red chilli/chile, deseeded and sliced
a handful of basil leaves, torn
a large handful of flat leaf parsley, finely chopped
1 teaspoon sugar
250 g/9 oz. sushi grade tuna, cut into 2.5-cm/1-inch cubes
200 g/7 oz. dried pasta or 160 g /6 oz. fresh pasta
1 tablespoon cracked black peppercorns
salt and freshly ground black pepper

SERVES 2

Heat 2 tablespoons of the oil in a heavy-bottomed pan. Add the garlic slices, anchovies and dried chilli flakes/hot red pepper flakes. When the garlic begins to colour and the anchovies have melted, add the onion and sauté until glassy and softened.

Add the capers and tomato purée/paste and deglaze the pan with the wine.

Add the tomatoes, chilli/chile, basil, parsley and sugar, and season with salt and black pepper. Stir well and leave to cook, half-covered, on a very, very low heat. Stir regularly to avoid the bottom catching (add a splash of water to let the sauce down if it looks too thick). When the tomatoes have almost broken down and you have a rich sauce, check for seasoning, remove from the heat and set aside.

Toss the tuna cubes in the cracked black pepper to very lightly coat them.

Start to cook the pasta in plenty of boiling salted water (see pages 20–21) according to the instructions on the packet.

While your pasta is boiling, heat 2 tablespoons of the remaining oil in a frying pan/skillet with the remaining squashed garlic halves. When the garlic begins to colour, add the tuna cubes, season with salt and black pepper and sear the top and bottom (two sides) on a high heat, but do not cook them right through. Remove from the heat, slice in half and set aside.

Drain the pasta, but keep a cup of the cooking water. Tip the hot drained pasta into the tomato sauce, add a small splash of the retained pasta cooking water and the rest of the olive oil. Toss with gusto over a high heat until the pasta is well coated and creamy.

Serve immediately topped with the seared tuna cubes and a little more freshly ground black pepper.

SHOWN HERE WITH PICI PASTA

MEAT & POULTRY

The quickest way to turn any pasta into a complete and substantial family meal is the addition of meat. Traditionally offcuts and leftovers were finely chopped or minced and slow-cooked with tomato, wine and herbs to create rich and filling sauces. Top this with a sprinkling of grated Parmesan and you are delivering a winner to the table. This section includes all my family favourites and more. Not all these recipes require hours of slow cooking, it is just as easy to bring out flavours with a little pancetta or bacon.

bologness

Classic Bolognese ragù has many ingredients that make up its magic. This is a pumped version of traditional Bolognese, which I have packed with umami.

2 tablespoons olive oil, plus extra for drizzling
80 g/½ cup diced pancetta
150 g/5½ oz. chopped portobello or chestnut/cremini mushrooms
1 onion, very finely chopped
1 carrot, grated
1 celery stick, very finely chopped
2 garlic cloves, crushed
450 g/1 lb. minced/ground beef
1 teaspoon dried oregano
3 bay leaves
400 g/14 oz. can chopped tomatoes or whole San Marzano
125 ml/½ cup red wine
60 ml/¼ cup marsala (optional)
125 ml/½ cup beef stock
4 tablespoons tomato purée/paste
2 anchovy fillets
600 g/21 oz. dried pasta or 480 g/18 oz. fresh pasta
salt and freshly ground black pepper
finely grated Parmigiano Reggiano, to serve
a knob/pat of butter, to serve

SERVES 6

SHOWN HERE WITH SPAGHETTI

Heat the oil in a large frying pan/skillet and fry the pancetta and mushrooms for 3–4 minutes until browned and the fat of the pancetta is rendered. Add the onion, carrot, celery and garlic, and sauté on a low heat, stirring regularly, until the vegetables have begun to give off their liquid, soften and caramelize slightly. Be patient with this stage, as waiting for the vegetables to cook down and caramelize properly will add a beautiful depth of flavour to the meat.

Add the minced/ground beef to the pan and cook, stirring regularly, until browned. Add the oregano, bay leaves, tomatoes, red wine, marsala (if using), stock, tomato purée/paste and anchovy fillets. Bring to the boil and then lower the heat, cover and simmer on a very low heat for 25–45 minutes (if you have time, you can let this simmer for up to 3 hours; basically the longer the better).

Towards the end of the cooking time, cook the pasta in plenty of salted boiling water (see pages 20–21) according to the packet instructions, then drain.

Taste and adjust the Bolognese seasoning (this won't need much salt), and drizzle in some extra olive oil to finish.

Toss the meat sauce through the pasta and serve topped with grated Parmigiano cheese and a knob/pat of butter.

SHOWN
HERE WITH
SPIRALIZED
BUTTERNUT
SQUASH

quick ragù

This is my grandmother's recipe and is about as easy and tasty as it gets. Loaded with umami, the seared meat and concentrated tomato purée/paste, enhanced by the wine and garlic, combine to create a ragù to die for. I have to be careful not to eat it all while 'tasting' for seasoning. It is a meatier olive oil-based ragù, not the better known juicy tomato-based Bolognese. This was what my Nonna Pasqua considered fast food!

5 tablespoons olive oil
1 garlic clove, peeled, squashed and halved lengthways
1 onion, sliced into 8 wedges
500 g/1 lb. 2 oz. minced/ground beef
1 large bay leaf
3 tablespoons tomato purée/paste
125 ml/½ cup red or white wine
600 g/21 oz. boodles or
600 g/21 oz. dried pasta or 320–480 g/12–18 oz. fresh pasta
salt and freshly ground black pepper
Parmigiano Reggiano shavings, to serve

SERVES 4

Heat the oil in a heavy-bottomed pan. Add the garlic and onion wedges. When these are sizzling, add the meat and seal it over a moderate-high heat until well browned all over.

Season with salt and black pepper and add the bay leaf and tomato purée/paste. Cook on a low heat, stirring regularly to prevent the bottom burning, until the oil begins to separate from the sauce.

Add the wine to the sauce and cook for a further 5 minutes, or until the wine has been absorbed.

Towards the end of cooking time cook the boodles or the pasta (see pages 20–21) according to the packet instructions.

Serve the quick ragù with the cooked, drained pasta or boodles and top with Parmigiano shavings and plenty of extra black pepper.

TASTY TRANSFORMATION

For a juicy Bolognese, add two 400 g/14-oz. cans chopped tomatoes and a pinch of dried oregano. Or better still, add enough Classic Red Sauce (page 25) to give the consistency required. A good-quality tomato sauce from a jar could also be added with excellent results.

amatriciana

The iconic Amatriciana sauce is traditionally made with guanciale (cured pork cheek), pecorino and tomatoes. If you cannot find guanciale, it is perfectly respectable to use pancetta or bacon as I do. I actually prefer bacon as I like my Amatriciana to be less fatty. Traditionally, you are supposed to toss in the pecorino as you combine the pasta with the sauce but I prefer mine on top.

4 tablespoons extra virgin olive oil
125 g/4½ oz. guanciale or smoked back bacon, cut into strips
2 garlic cloves, finely chopped
1 onion, thinly sliced
a splash of red wine
½ teaspoon dried chilli flakes/hot red pepper flakes (optional)
½ teaspoon dried oregano
400 g/14 oz. can tomatoes or whole San Marzano (if using whole ones, squash them through your fingers)
1 teaspoon sugar
200 g/7 oz. dried pasta or 160 g/6 oz. fresh pasta
salt and freshly ground black pepper
2 tablespoons finely grated pecorino, to serve

SERVES 2

Heat 2 tablespoons of the olive oil in a heavy-bottomed pan. Add the bacon and toss until it is sizzling and begins to take colour. Add the garlic and onion and stir well.

When the onion has softened, deglaze the pan with the wine and leave to sizzle for a minute. Leave to bubble for a couple more minutes to allow some of the alcohol to burn off, then add the dried chilli flakes/hot red pepper flakes (if using), oregano, tomatoes and sugar. Stir well and season with a little salt and black pepper.

Cook half-covered on a medium-low heat for around 15–20 minutes, until rich and tasty.

Towards the end of the cooking time, cook the pasta in plenty of boiling salted water (see pages 20–21) according to the instructions on the packet.

Drain the pasta, but keep a cup of the cooking water. Tip the hot drained pasta into the bacon sauce, adding a small splash of the retained pasta cooking water and the remaining 2 tablespoons of olive oil. Toss with gusto over a high heat until the pasta is well coated and creamy.

Serve immediately with plenty of extra freshly ground black pepper and the finely grated pecorino cheese.

SHOWN HERE WITH BUCATINI PASTA

SHOWN HERE WITH PENNONI PASTA

sausage & tomato

This is a really versatile and classic Italian recipe. You can create a 'white' version of this by swapping red wine for white wine, and the tomatoes for a couple of handfuls of broccoli florets. Season with ½ teaspoon fennel seeds, unless the sausages are already seasoned with fennel. A splash of double/heavy cream can be added to both versions for a creamy edition.

Equally, a quick creamy, spicy sausage mix solution can be found in moments by mixing a tablespoon of 'nduja with a sautéed onion, a splash of wine and around 300 ml/1¼ cups double/heavy cream. All versions are mouth-watering and should be topped with copious amounts of finely grated cheese and ground black pepper.

2 tablespoons extra virgin olive oil
1 onion, thinly sliced
2 garlic cloves, finely chopped
400 g/14 oz. tasty sausage meat, preferably Italian*
a sprig of rosemary, leaves only, finely chopped
½ tablespoon tomato purée/paste
150 ml/⅔ cup red wine
400 g/14 oz. can chopped tomatoes or whole San Marzano tomatoes
½–1 teaspoon sugar
200 g/7 oz. dried pasta or 160 g/6 oz. fresh pasta
salt and freshly ground black pepper
2 tablespoons finely grated Parmigiano Reggiano or pecorino, to serve

***Buy regular sausages, remove the casing and use the meat.**

SERVES 2

Heat the olive oil in a heavy-bottomed pan. Add the onion and garlic and cook until the onion has softened. Add the sausage meat and break up into small pieces with the back of the spoon.

When the sausage meat is cooked through and sizzling, add the rosemary and tomato purée/paste and deglaze the pan with the wine. Leave to bubble for a couple of minutes to allow some of the alcohol to burn off, then add the tomatoes and sugar. Stir well and season with a little salt and black pepper.

Cook half-covered on a medium-low heat for around 15–20 minutes, until rich and tasty.

Towards the end of the cooking time, cook the pasta in plenty of boiling salted water (see pages 20–21) according to the instructions on the packet.

Drain the pasta, but keep a cup of the cooking water. Tip the hot drained pasta into the sausage sauce, adding a small splash of the retained pasta cooking water, and toss with gusto over a high heat until the pasta is well coated and creamy.

Serve immediately with plenty of extra freshly ground black pepper and the finely grated Parmigiano or pecorino cheese.

SHOWN
HERE WITH
SPAGHETTI

crispy gravy spaghetti

Pan juices from a roast make one of the most flavourful sauces ever.

1.8 kg/4 lb. roasting chicken, preferably free-range or organic, skin patted dry with a paper towel
3 onions, cut into wedges
3 sprigs of rosemary
3 sprigs of thyme
1 whole head garlic, top sliced off
a good glug extra virgin olive oil
250 ml/1 cup white wine
1 tablespoon tomato purée/paste
1 chicken stock cube
1 tablespoon grated Parmigiano Reggiano, to serve
500 g/1 lb. 2 oz. dried spaghetti
salt and freshly ground black pepper

a roasting pan only just bigger than your chicken, otherwise the juices will all evaporate

SERVES 4–6

Preheat the oven to 200°C (400°F) Gas 6.

Place two onion wedges inside the cavity of the chicken along with a sprig of rosemary and thyme. Place the rest of the onion wedges in the bottom of the roasting pan.

Sit the chicken on top, add the garlic and massage a little olive oil into the chicken. Pour a glug of oil on the onion around the chicken. Season everything with salt and pepper.

Roast in the preheated oven for 10 minutes, then turn the heat down to 180°C (350°F) Gas 4. Pour the wine around the chicken (not onto it) and roast for a further 1 hour and 20 minutes for a 1.8 kg/4 lb. chicken, or until the juices run clear.

In the last half hour of cooking, bring a large pan of salted water to the boil for the pasta.

Remove the cooked chicken from the roasting pan, place on a dish, cover in foil and leave to rest.

Set the oven temperature to 220°C (420°F) Gas 7.

Place the roasting pan over a low heat and deglaze. If necessary add another splash of wine, you should have about 1 cm/½ inch of gravy in the bottom of the pan.

Add the tomato purée/paste and stock cube. As soon as the sauce looks rich and glossy remove from the heat and stir in the Parmigiano cheese.

Cook the spaghetti in the salted boiling water for 4 minutes only (the usual cooking time is 12 minutes). Tip the hot drained pasta into the roasting pan and toss with gusto over a high heat until well coated in the gravy.

Spread evenly in the pan and return to the oven. Cook for 10 minutes at 220°C (420°F) Gas 7, then reduce the temperature to 200°C (400°F) Gas 6 for a further 10 minutes, or until bits of the pasta are crispy and the rest is al dente but not tough.

Place the rested roast chicken on top of the crispy pasta. Pour over any resting juices and serve. If you like, you can take the pasta out 5 minutes early, place the chicken on top and return to the oven to crisp up the chicken skin before serving.

duck & red wine ragù

This ragù is delicious on pasta with orange and Parmigiano gremolata as shown here, but equally good on cheesy polenta. You can also cook this in a slow cooker on high for 3–4 hours or low for 6–8 hours.

4 duck legs, skin and fat removed
1 tablespoon olive oil
1 large onion, finely diced
1 celery stick, finely diced
1 carrot, finely diced
3 large garlic cloves, crushed
2 tablespoons tomato purée/paste
2 chicken stock cubes
400–600 g/14–21 oz. dried pasta or 320–480 g/12–18 oz. fresh pasta
salt and freshly ground black pepper

FOR THE RED WINE MARINADE
1 celery stick
a bunch of thyme
3 sprigs of rosemary
2 bay leaves
10 juniper berries, crushed
1 bottle red wine

SERVES 4–6

Cut away the meat from the duck leg bones. Set the bones to one side and dice the meat into 2.5-cm/1-inch pieces.

Start by preparing the marinade. To make a bouquet garni, cut the celery stalk in two, sandwich the herbs in-between the two ribs and tie together with cooking string/twine. Place the diced meat, bones, bouquet garni and juniper berries in a sealable container, cover with some of the red wine and leave to marinate in the fridge overnight or up to 24 hours. Reserve the rest of the bottle of wine.

Note: you can skip the marinade day and simply add the bouquet garni, juniper berries and bottle of red wine to the pot when cooking.

When you are ready to cook the duck, drain the wine from the marinated duck into a container and set aside. Keep the bouquet garni, bones and juniper berries with the meat.

Heat the oil in a heavy-bottomed pan. Brown the duck pieces and bones and set aside. Add the onion, celery, carrot and garlic to the pan and cook until the vegetables begin to soften and the onion is translucent. Return the browned meat, bones, bits of juniper and bouquet garni to the pan and deglaze with the reserved marinade.

Add the tomato purée/paste, the rest of the red wine from the bottle and the stock cubes. Season with salt and black pepper.

Bring to a simmer, then lower the heat and cover. Cook on low for 1½–2 hours. (You can also cook in the oven at 180°C (350°F) Gas 4 for 1– 1½ hours.) If the bottom starts to catch, add a little stock or wine. Remove the bones and bouquet garni before serving.

Cook the pasta in plenty of boiling salted water (see pages 20–21) according to the packet instructions. Drain the pasta, but keep a cup of the cooking water. Tip the hot drained pasta into the ragù, adding a splash of the pasta cooking water. Toss with gusto over a high heat until the pasta is well coated and creamy. Serve immediately.

TASTY TOPPER *the grated zest of 2 oranges, a large handful of finely chopped flat leaf parsley and 3 tablespoons Parmigiano, mixed.*

SHOWN HERE WITH
RIGATONI PASTA

white veal ragù

This is one of those recipes that if executed properly could gain you a standing ovation at the table. This milky cousin of the more familiar tomato-based, slow-cooked meat sauces is out of this world and well worth the slow cook.

3 tablespoons olive oil
500 g/1 lb. 2 oz. minced/ground veal (not too lean, it works better with a bit of fat)
3 garlic cloves, finely chopped
2 sprigs of rosemary, leaves only, finely chopped
6 sage leaves, finely chopped
1 onion, finely chopped
1 carrot, finely chopped
1 celery stick, finely chopped
250 ml/1 cup white wine
1 litre/quart semi-skimmed milk
1 bay leaf
a pinch of freshly grated nutmeg
400–600 g/14–21 oz. dried pasta or 320–480 g/12–18 oz. fresh pasta
30 g/¼ stick butter
salt and freshly ground black pepper
4 tablespoons finely grated Parmigiano Reggiano, to serve

SERVES 4–6

Heat the olive oil in a heavy-bottomed pan, add the minced/ground veal and stir until it becomes golden and browned.

Add the garlic, rosemary and sage and leave to cook for 3–4 minutes. Add the onion, carrot and celery and cook for another 5 minutes until softened, stirring regularly to ensure the mixture does not catch on the bottom.

Add the wine and cook off the alcohol for a couple of minutes. Add half the milk in one go, then add the rest of the milk a little at a time until the milk is completely absorbed. Add the bay leaf and nutmeg. Season with salt and black pepper. Half-cover and cook on a very, very low heat for 1–2 hours or until reduced to a rich and tasty sauce.

Towards the end of the cooking time, cook the pasta in plenty of boiling salted water (see pages 20–21) according to the instructions on the packet.

Drain the pasta, but keep a cup of the cooking water. Tip the hot drained pasta into the veal ragù, adding a small splash of the retained pasta cooking water and the butter. Toss with gusto over a high heat until the pasta is well coated and creamy.

Serve immediately with plenty of extra freshly ground black pepper and the finely grated Parmigiano cheese.

SHOWN HERE WITH FUSILLI PASTA

chicken liver & sage

This recipe is one of my favourites; the creamy livers with the punchy sage are delicate and sublime. It is important to use very fresh chicken livers and to ensure that they are properly cooked through.

2 tablespoons extra virgin olive oil
2 garlic cloves, squashed, peeled and halved lengthways
1 onion, thinly sliced
400 g/14 oz. chicken livers, rinsed, dried and roughly chopped
a sprig of thyme, leaves only, or 4 sage leaves
125 ml/½ cup brandy or white wine
a splash of chicken stock, if needed
200 g/7 oz. dried pasta or 160 g/6 oz. fresh pasta
70 g/5 tablespoons butter
salt and freshly ground black pepper
4 tablespoons finely grated Parmigiano Reggiano, to serve

SERVES 2

Put a large pan of salted water on to boil for the pasta following the instructions on pages 20–21.

Meanwhile, heat the olive oil in a heavy-bottomed pan. Add the garlic and onion and stir well. Turn down the heat and sauté until the onion has softened.

When the onion begins to colour, turn up the heat and add the chicken livers and herbs. Season with salt and pepper, add the brandy and sauté briefly until the livers are cooked through, about 4–5 minutes. If it looks like the onions are burning, add a splash of chicken stock. Once the alcohol has evaporated, remove from the heat and set aside.

When the salted water is at a rolling boil, add the pasta and cook according to the instructions on the packet.

Drain the pasta, but keep a cup of the cooking water. Tip the hot drained pasta into the chicken livers, adding a small splash of the retained pasta cooking water and the butter. Toss with gusto over a high heat until the pasta is well coated and creamy.

Serve immediately with plenty of extra freshly ground black pepper and the finely grated Parmigiano cheese.

alla gricia

Known as the precursor to the Amatriciana recipe (page 154), Alla Gricia is a pasta sauce from Lazio made with cured pork cheeks, pecorino Romano and plenty of black pepper.

2 tablespoons olive oil
150 g/5½ oz. guanciale or unsmoked back bacon, cut into strips
½ teaspoon freshly ground black pepper, plus extra to serve
200 g/7 oz. dried pasta or 160 g/6 oz. fresh pasta
3 tablespoons finely grated pecorino

SERVES 2

SHOWN HERE WITH RIGATONI PASTA

Put a large pan of salted water on to boil for the pasta following the instructions on pages 20–21.

Meanwhile, heat the olive oil in a heavy-bottomed pan, add the bacon and sauté over a medium heat until it becomes golden and browned, but not burnt. Add the black pepper, combine well and turn off the heat.

When the salted water is at a rolling boil, add the pasta and cook according to the packet instructions.

Drain the pasta, but keep a cup of the cooking water. Tip the hot drained pasta into the bacon, adding a splash of the retained pasta cooking water and the pecorino cheese. Toss with gusto over a high heat until the pasta is well coated and creamy.

Serve immediately with plenty of extra freshly ground black pepper.

alfredo

Alfredo is the king of the fresh pasta sauces and a firm international favourite. This dish can also be described as a 'heart attack on a plate'! It was invented in Rome, at a restaurant called Alfredo alla Scrofa (which, incidentally, means 'at the south'). This creamy delight was served by the restaurant owner, Alfredo, with a gold spoon and fork given to him by Douglas Fairbanks and Mary Pickford while on their honeymoon in 1927. Spinach (green) fettuccine is synonymous with Alfredo all over Italy, but this deliciously rich sauce makes anything it coats wonderful. I have served it here with a couple of handfuls of leftover cooked chicken and fresh green tagliatelle.

200 ml/generous ¾ cup double/heavy cream
125 g/1 stick very fresh butter
a good pinch of freshly grated nutmeg
75 g/1 cup grated Parmigiano Reggiano cheese (or half Parmigiano Reggiano and half pecorino cheese)
200 g/7 oz. cooked chicken pieces
200 g/7 oz. dried pasta or 160 g/6 oz. fresh pasta
salt and freshly ground black pepper

SERVES 2

Put a large pan of salted water on to boil for the pasta following the instructions on pages 20–21.

Meanwhile, to make the sauce, heat the cream, butter and nutmeg in a heavy-bottomed pan over a medium heat for about 2–3 minutes, stirring occasionally, until the butter has melted into the cream.

Stir in the cheese and chicken, heat through and then remove from the heat. If the sauce is a little too runny, heat over a low heat until it is thickened. Season carefully – this dish rarely needs salt as the cheese imparts enough.

When the salted water is at a rolling boil, add the pasta and cook according to the packet instructions.

Drain the pasta, but keep a cup of the cooking water. Tip the hot drained pasta into the sauce, adding a splash of the retained pasta cooking water. Toss with gusto over a high heat until the pasta looks well coated and creamy.

Serve immediately with plenty of extra freshly ground black pepper.

SHOWN HERE WITH FRESH SPINACH TAGLIATELLE

meatballs

This iconic classic Italian-American dish is a hybrid of the dainty meatballs made in Southern Italy and the huge meatballs featured in that unforgettable 'Lady and the Tramp' spaghetti scene.

FOR THE MEATBALLS

- 1 thick slice of white bread, crusts removed
- 5–6 tablespoons milk
- 30 g/¼ stick butter
- 1 small onion, finely chopped
- 1 garlic clove, crushed
- 450 g/1 lb. minced/ground beef
- 50 g/2 oz. prosciutto crudo, very finely chopped
- 2 tablespoons finely grated Parmigiano Reggiano
- 1 tablespoon tomato ketchup or tomato purée/paste
- 1 UK large/US extra-large egg, beaten
- a handful of flat leaf parsley, finely chopped
- salt and freshly ground black pepper
- plain/all-purpose flour, for dusting
- olive oil, for frying

TO SERVE
Classic Red Sauce (page 25) or good store-bought sauce
400–600 g/14–21 oz. dried pasta or 320–480 g/12–18 oz. fresh pasta
20 g/1½ tablespoons butter
4 tablespoons finely grated Parmigiano Reggiano

SERVES 4–6

For the meatballs, soak the bread in the milk, enough to make it soft but not sloppy.

Melt the butter in a non-stick frying pan/skillet, add the onion and garlic and fry until soft and glassy and beginning to colour. Place all the other meatball ingredients (except the soaked bread) in a large mixing bowl, add the fried onion mixture and use your hands to work all the ingredients together. Add enough or all of the soaked bread to make a meatball consistency.

Check the seasoning by frying off a teaspoon of the mixture in the frying pan/skillet. Adjust the seasoning if necessary and mix well.

Dust your hands with a little flour and roll the mixture into meatballs between the palms of your hands (about 4 cm/1½ inch in diameter) and place on a baking sheet ready to fry.

Heat about 2.5 cm/1 inch of olive oil in a heavy-bottomed pan and shallow-fry the meatballs until browned on all sides. Turn gently and, when cooked, place onto paper towels to soak up any excess oil.

Place the meatballs into a wide-bottomed pan and cover in two-thirds of the red tomato sauce. Cover and cook on a very low heat for about 20–30 minutes.

Alternatively, you can bake the meatballs and red sauce together in an oven preheated to 190°C (375°F) Gas 5.

Towards the end of the cooking time, cook the pasta in plenty of salted boiling water (see pages 20–21) according to the packet instructions, then drain. While the pasta is cooking, gently heat the remaining red tomato sauce and set aside.

Drain the pasta, but keep a cup of the cooking water. Tip the hot drained pasta into the heated red tomato sauce, adding a small splash of the retained pasta cooking water and the butter. Toss with gusto over a high heat until the pasta is well coated and creamy.

Serve the pasta in individual bowls and spoon over the meatballs. Serve immediately with the Parmigiano cheese and plenty of extra freshly ground black pepper.

index